JOURNEY TO REDEMPTION

RYAN T. MOORER

FIREBRAND
PUBLISHING

CONTENTS

PREFACE

"God won't put no more on you than you can bear." I have heard that scripture all my life. It's easy to say for those who ain't never been through shit. The truth is *all* tests, all trials and all suffering feels like it's "more than you can bear."

Hate is weight. Too heavy to walk with, too heavy to hold, and too heavy to productively function with. Hate is not just heavy, but it is also darkness. It is the darkness of depression, of worry and pain. We try our best to function as we walk hunched over in a fog of instability and uncertainty. A fog of wondering "when will life be normal again." Eventually, we realize on the other side of vulnerability is strength. On the other side of pain is relief. On the other side of disappointment is clarity. Momma used to say, "Everyone has to cross fool's mountain." Sometimes the journey across that mountain takes a long time, but eventually we cross it.

My journey began when I was wide-eyed and trusted the world. My voyage was a winding road of mistrust, failure, heartbreak, and growth. My stepdad was an abusive man. His rage was terrifying. He never pretended to be anything other than a cruel man. My pastor, however, was different. He was a manipulator and a con. I never believed in my stepdad because I knew who he was. I believed in Pastor Rudders, and I later learned that was part of his con. He fooled me into thinking he had my best interests at heart, and I hated him for that. That hatred turned into rage. A rage so strong that the only way to satisfy my thirst for revenge was by killing the Pastor.

CHAPTER ONE

I learned how to manipulate people from a young age going to church. Pastor Rudders Prangles always put on a show. I watched him watch people. He told his congregation of eager listeners what they needed to hear. "You'll be healed," "You'll be blessed," "Your change is coming." He would spout clichés that ignited a swell of enthusiasm and excitement as music would blare and bodies would dance in the isles.

My mother came to Trueway Church the summer of 1990. She was in an abusive relationship that had caused her many sleepless nights. She walked in with her five boys and filed into the back pew. I'm the second oldest of my brothers. Ron was fourteen, I was twelve, LJ was six, Marc was four and Mell, the youngest, was only three. We stood there in that gutted, double wide mobile home, dressed in our khaki pants, white starched shirts, and buster brown shoes in Bamberg, South Carolina. Momma had been fighting the night before, her dark skin puffy around her eyes. Momma was a strong woman, but she carried her pain in her face. She always looked like she wanted to cry but refused to ever let her children see her tears. Her eyes had the slightest hint of a gray ring around the pupils. Her face carried her fatigue. She had lost many fights. But she was a proud Christian woman. She was a product of old school salvation. The kind that stayed there till "death do you part." The kind that prayed until change came. The kind that loved hard and hurt harder. Many nights we could hear her through the thin walls of our three-bedroom apartment, praying after she had fasted all day. She had a beautiful voice and always started out prayer with,

"I know somehow, I know some way, we're going to make it. No matter what the test or whatever comes our way, we're going to make it. With Jesus on our side, things will work out fine. We're going to make it."

And there she stayed, on her knees praying and praying, calling out to Jesus until the tongues came. There she stayed until the spirit took hold of her, moving her body in praise and dance, slaying her in the spirit, breaking her, exhausting her until her body slumped over, reducing her to tears. Then she would get up, ready to face another day, renewed in faith but still tired. She wanted something better for her children. She wanted something better for herself. She was tired of fighting at night then getting up to see her children off to school in the morning; tired of her body aching and stiff every morning; weary of fixing meals in the dark because the lights were off again; shattered from pleading for this man to stop hitting her while muffling her cries so that her children wouldn't hear her torment and pain; disgusted from the smell of Schlitz malt liquor beer and Newport cigarettes lying next to her; fed up with the broken promises and countless extra women; frightened from the thought of what type of men these five boys were going to be with the example that lived at home. She prayed every day that God would intervene and save her boys from following the path of their live-in example. She prayed for a better illustration of a man.

That was how we found ourselves in the back of that church listening to God's word from Rudders Prangles.

It seemed like he could smell her concerns. He was very observant. All predators are. He walked over to us and smiled in a way that made us feel comfortable. I was amazed. Never had I seen a man that didn't drink or smoke, and he still took care of his own family. He was the first man that I had ever known who didn't have children outside his marriage. He had a job, a real job that he kept year-round, unlike my stepdad who quit every few months. We sat there and watched as he looked at my mom in her face and told her, "God hears your prayers."

She burst into tears. It was as if she had finally gotten confirmation that all of her suffering and pain would soon end. I remember how she cried and cried. I remember thinking about how different things were going to be now that God had heard her prayers. We all cried. My mom laid her head down in the palms of her hands. The other mothers and missionaries rushed to her with towels. They stood her up as the Pastor reached for the olive oil bottle. He unscrewed the top, poured it into his hands, rubbed them together and anointed her forehead. The oiled trickled down the side of her face as he prayed over her.

"Father God in the name of Jesus, once more again we come before you with bowed heads and humbled hearts."

She looked renewed. Someone started clapping loudly. The drummer grabbed his sticks and began a hand clapping rhythm. The organist and the bass guitar player followed suit. And Momma danced. She danced and danced and danced. The Pastor walked over to all five of us and grabbed us all, anointing us all with oil. We jumped up and down, not really on rhythm, not sure what we were jumping for. But we jumped. Momma, on the other hand, glided across the floor. She had an angelic spirit that made us sit back and watch as she moved. She seemed to be with the angels. We left the church that day and went home with great expectations. Momma was happy. I hadn't seen her smile in a long time, but nothing had changed.

CHAPTER TWO

We came home from church that day to find my stepdad waiting at the door. He was a big man, standing over six feet tall. He towered above us all. His presence was intimidating. He had light brown skin with a mini afro that he hadn't let go from the 70's. He was a hard man, hardened from his father and his childhood. He didn't finish high school, so he was put to work at an early age. The calluses on his hands were from years of working in his father's cotton and tobacco fields. He was an angry man, angry at the way the world had unjustly shit on him. It had cheated him, toyed with him. He never had enough education, but he had the skill. He was strong but not young enough. He was the perfect fit but didn't read well. He could count but couldn't write. His life was filled with buts and almost's or close but not quite's. And that was the source of his rage. It was a quiet rage, one that he controlled until that rage built up and he exploded in uncontrollable violence. He loved the fear of others and we were all afraid of him.

We entered the apartment, and he immediately and quietly asked,

"Who stays at church this late?"

The softness in his voice was unnerving. We had all experienced the quiet buildup of his

uncontrollable violence. Momma looked at him and said,

"We didn't have a ride, Harry."

"So, you expect me to cook my own dinner?" he asked.

She paused before she answered him. She knew that the wrong tone

would be construed as disrespect in front of the children.

"No, Harry. I took something out and it won't take long to make," she said.

My stepdad sat down in his favorite chair, flipping the channels between football games. No one said anything. We knew better. Our place was in our room, quiet. And that's where we went. All five of us tip toed up those stairs and piled into our bedroom. We sat on the floor with our legs crossed, Indian style, playing Connect Four. My stepdad was quiet too, silent while he drank beer after beer. Soundless while his imagination mixed with the alcohol, pushing him into a delusional state.

"You must got a new man at that church!" he yelled.

My mother started to hum her prayer song, Myrna

Summers' *We're Gonna Make It*. Her melodious voice drowned out the mad scoffs of my stepfather. She called us down to dinner and we saw the tears in her eyes. The tears of expectation. The tears of foreknowing that this night would be like so many other nights.

I looked at her and asked, "What's wrong, Ma?"

Her response was in song. *"With Jesus on our side, things will work out fine, we're gonna make it."*

She leaned down and kissed my dimples. Her tears dampened my face. I sat down at the table and ate my dinner in silence.

Later that night, I awoke to the sound of shattered glass and an angry scream.

"Who stays in church that long?" he yelled.

It was the drunken rage of my stepdad. Quickly, I jumped out of bed and blindly ran towards the light pouring out from the cracks of their bedroom door.

"Stop!" I screamed.

I was now standing witness to a horrible scene, a nightmare that wasn't a dream but too often a fixture of my reality. There stood my stepdad, holding his hand in a threatening grip around momma's neck as she grasped for air and cringed in pain.

"Let her go! You're hurting her!" I screamed.

"I'm just showing your mother something. Go back to bed," he asserted.

Did he think I was an idiot? Did he think I was stupid? I

could see shards of broken glass in the room. I ran towards him and tried to pry his fastened fingers from her neck. I was a child. Small and scared. He batted me away with ease and flung her to the floor. I ran back to her side as he straddled her. I felt helpless knowing that he would just swat me away again. I jumped on his back, trying desperately to pull him backwards as my mother struggled to get out from under him. He released his grip as I bit down on his shoulder. He threw me off his back and stormed out of the room, and for an instant I thought the nightmare was over. Within seconds, he came back into the room with his thick leather black belt wrapped around his fist, swinging it wildly in anger and screaming that he would teach me a lesson. Momma did her best to shield me from the blows, absorbing most of the abuse. When he had exhausted himself, he left. Momma was hurt but she tended to my wounds first. I wanted to ask her why, I wanted to ask her "How could he?"

She saw the questions in my eyes and answered them simply.

"He's your daddy and you have to love him. God wants you to love him."

I laid in my bed that night thinking that the Pastor had lied. Nothing had changed.

I watched Momma endure abuse both physically and mentally, all the while telling her five boys to love and respect their dad. I didn't want to love him, but I did. I didn't want to respect him, but I had to. Doing the right thing vindicated my mom. With each beating, I discovered that my fear of him gradually slipped away. With each beating came a promise of change. Each beating ended with him asking for repentance and a second chance. My stepdad's empty promises along with Pastor Rudders' manipulation through scriptures was partially why she stayed.

The other reason she stayed was for her boys. Her boys, her five boys. She thought she was doing what was best for us. A day would barely pass before the sound of forceful strikes and gut-wrenching cries echoed throughout the house. Sunday after Sunday, she would gather herself, get dressed, and take us to church. Some days when it was just my mom and us in the house, she would become so overwhelmed with fear, anxiety, and loneliness that she would suddenly burst into tears. We watched her. We saw her pain. We knew why she hurt. We saw her in the prayer line every Sunday, waiting for the Pastor to tell her to leave, but all she got was

"And unto the married I command, [yet] not I, but the Lord, let not the wife depart from [her] husband," (**1 Corinthians 7:10-17**) or *"And if a woman shall put away her husband, and be married to another, she committeth adultery,"* (**Mark 10:12**).

Looking back, all she got from Pastor Prangles was scripture and a bunch of sob stories about needing another vehicle or a new suit or a new riding lawn mower. It hurt to know that she was suffering and that all this "Man of God" could offer was a forehead wet from cheap olive oil, a chance to shout on sore bruised legs, and an opportunity to buy his wife a new hat. It hurt to know that every time she spoke to the Pastor, the only advice he could give was one of his many tired clichés.

"Hold on and don't let go."

"Weeping may endure for a night, but joy comes in the morning."

"He may not come when you want him, but he's always on time."

He never told her to leave. He never told her to protect herself. He never told her to take her family and run. All he did was yell and give us his cliché's. Who needs a fucking cliché when your eyes are swollen and your lip is busted?

My stepdad beat us the same way he did Momma. I preferred the beatings to hearing the hurtful sounds of him using my mother as his punching bag. Sometimes I stood at the bedroom door when he came home. Usually I just shook like a leaf trying to hold onto its branch during a brisk fall breeze. It seemed like every Saturday night before church and Sunday after church, my stepdad was in that crazy-ass way, blaming Momma for everything. Everything was Momma's fault. She couldn't do anything right. When he started, she took things to the bedroom and closed the door to spare us from seeing her battered.

I hated my stepdad as much as I loved him. The contradiction was painful. The hardest part was trying to understand Momma. I didn't understand why she let my stepdad treat her like that. Why was she always praying? Why did she keep saying to trust in God? If she couldn't stand up for herself, how would she protect us? What happens to us when he kills her? I didn't want to believe he would kill my brothers and me, but I couldn't be sure. We couldn't possibly defend ourselves against a strong man like my stepdad, especially not when he was in one of his rages. But mom stayed, trusting, hoping and waiting for a change, believing that each prayer she received was the one that would make all her hurt go away.

We stayed in that church for years. Each Sunday was a buildup of emotions. High spirited praise, shouting, jumping and dancing. Nothing changed. We were told each Sunday that life would be different if we danced long enough or cried hard enough. We sat there each week believing every word that was uttered from the mouth of this pastor. Momma gave everything, hoping that the beatings would stop, that the lies would cease, and that the pain would end. Because of her faith, she sacrificed money for bills and even gave portions of her income tax returns. Years of putting more and more money into Pastor Prangles pocket. And whenever we failed at anything, it wasn't because of his advice. It was because of our shortcomings and our lack of faith. Pastor Prangles twisted the Bible and the image of God into something ugly and frightening. Most of the time, he just wanted to step on us, to grind his Christian truth into us with the heel of his $400 Wing-Tip Oxford Salvatore Ferragamo shoes. It was years before I became so disgusted by the hate radiating from this pastor that I would leave. He made me sick. And I thought to myself if that's what being a Christian is, then I wanted nothing, absolutely nothing, to do with it. That was also the beginning of the turning point for Momma.

CHAPTER THREE

I loved and hated my stepdad. I saw other dads in my neighborhood. They were everywhere, with mustaches and wearing Hawaiian shirts, carrying wallets and drinking beers. They were at family gatherings, throwing the ball to their sons, teaching them about life and love, showing them the right way to do things. On TV, Dad's gave stumbling advice or blathered into obnoxious temper tantrums, flaunting their cosmic ineptitude while watching the flames of the charcoal grill. Sitcom dads were teased by wives and taunted by children until the moment of crisis when violins would swell and fatherly advice was dished out like alcohol for a skinned knee. It hurt but it was good.

The dads I met in real life showed up for football games and school plays. My stepdad was not one of them. I wondered if all dads acted the way mine did behind closed doors. I wondered if my friends' mothers cried at night. After a while, I did what my mom did and acted as if the beatings didn't happen. I'd pretend that we were just like everyone else, a happy family with five great kids. But it was hard to pretend after witnessing the most brutal of my stepdad's beatings which was Mom's final straw.

It was a cool Sunday morning. I remember that day clearly. The house felt different. Momma was up early as usual, but my stepdad was up too. We only had one full bathroom in that apartment which made daily hygiene a struggle. We filed in one by one on rotation, each waiting eagerly for the next to finish, each thinking the person before him was taking way too long. This day was different. My stepdad disrupted the rotation. He was up shaving. I went in after he was done and could still smell his Old Spice aftershave. I wondered why he was up so early, but I didn't dare ask. We all rushed through our routines and got dressed. I was the last downstairs to breakfast and the last to notice my stepdad fully dressed. He had on a shirt and tie.

"OH, MY GOD, is he going to church?" Momma had a joyful expression in her eyes that could not be contained. It was all over her face. Her smile made all of us smile. Her joy gave us all joy. We sat down to grits, eggs and bacon for breakfast. Momma rushed upstairs to put on her dress.

After breakfast, we sat quietly in the living room waiting for her to come downstairs. This was the first time my stepdad ever wanted to come to church with us, and she wanted to look good. She wore an off-white top with a navy-blue skirt and matching jacket. Her shoes were nude. Momma loved her hats. She came downstairs proudly wearing a lightweight textured horsehair fabric, off white 2 1/2 inch turned down brim hat with silk flowers. Momma loved her hats. It was beautiful, and she wore it well.

We piled into his T-Top Cutlass and drove to church with a smile on our faces. The sultry summer day was hot and the air conditioner didn't work so my stepdad took the glass out of the roof. We entered the church and my stepdad walked in last, almost reluctantly. Momma sat in the middle row. Not her usual spot, but I figured she didn't want to make the old man too uncomfortable. We filed in beside them. The seven of us filled the entire pew. Church started like normal with devotional services, high spirited praise, dance and then the offering.

The Pastor always came out of his study right before the offering. He stood in the pulpit and said in his booming voice,

"Will a man rob God? Yet ye have robbed me. But ye say, wherein have we robbed thee? In tithes and offerings. Ye are cursed with a curse: for ye have robbed me." It was Malachi 3:8. It put the fear of God into all stingy givers. Then it was time for the sermon. Prangles stood in the pulpit and spoke to the church, lecturing the church on responsibilities and manhood.

"For also when we were with you, we enjoined you this,

that if any man does not like to work, neither let him eat 2 Thessalonians.

For if a man has not the art of ruling his house, how will he take care of the church of God? I Timothy 3:5."

And that's the way the entire service went. Minutes turned into hours of finger pointing and innuendos wrapped around, "God's Word" and "sound doctrine." I could feel my dad growing angrier by the minute. We all sat silently. Why would he antagonize my dad? Why was he poking the beast? When the service was over, Pastor Prangles stood there in his pretentious glory, thinking that he had delivered us from evil. We left the service in silence. My dad was quiet the entire way home. Almost immediately upon entering the house did the screams and the banging began. We knew the drill and quickly ran to our bedrooms. My younger brothers held their ears, waiting for the sounds to stop. But this time was different. Waiting for the silence, I heard the bedroom door slam and the sounds of footsteps rumbling down the hallway. Momma was trying to get away. The footsteps grew louder and closer. He was chasing her down the hall. I looked out to see him dragging her by the hair back into the bedroom. Momma was crying. I saw my stepdad lunge forward to grab her by the neck again, but she pulled back and screamed.

"Harry! Stop! Harry! Please!" I had never heard her sound so afraid. The bedroom door flew open and they spilled out into the hallways.

"Daddy's going to kill her," I said to my brothers.

"We have to do something."

I ran into the hallway and jumped on his back. Momma was half dressed, her blue and white top torn. Her legs were splayed wide open and my stepdad was straddling her, pummeling her with clenched fists. Each lick seemed to echo as he screamed, "WHAT DID YOU TELL THEM PEOPLE? WHY WAS YOU TALKING ABOUT ME!"

Every word out of his mouth was followed by a fist. Blood spurted from Momma's face. She started thrashing around, kicking her legs, holding up her arms to ward off the punches, trying to break free, trying to save herself. I was frozen in place, but then something inside of me took over, and I knew I had to do something. I felt no fear, only rage. I gouged at his eyes as my other brothers came running and screaming,

"Leave her alone! Stop punching my momma!"

He didn't turn around. He just kept punching, swatting us away like flies. The next thing I knew I was on my back absorbing wild blows. My two younger brothers jumped on his back, trying to pull him off. Sweat was dripping down his face and his eyes were glazed and wild. He paused, breathing heavy, looking down at me, bloody and crying. For a moment, I expected an apology. But it was as if I was looking into the eyes of a stranger. A stillness came over the room. The smell of blood and sweat was thick in the air.

That's when we heard a faint voice yell,

"I'm calling the cops." It was our neighbor next door.

My father looked stunned. It was as if he'd awakened from a bad dream. His head dropped, and his shoulders slumped. I looked over at Momma. Her eyes were purple, and her face was bloody. She didn't look back at me. My stepdad left after that day. Momma pressed charges. She never talked about the beatings.

The next Sunday was her last Sunday at church. She testified about the grueling ordeal that she had faced. She stood and talked about the worst experience of her life. All Prangles could muster was another tired ass cliché. "He may not come when you want him, but he's always on time."

All Momma's giving, shouting, crying, praying and fasting had amounted to ten years of the same situation. The beatings had taken their toll on her and she soon lost her vision because of them. The only answer that she ever got was her change hadn't come because her faith wasn't strong enough. The only change in her life was her slowly diminishing vision. Momma was done with this fake pastor and his bullshit ministry. She left because she knew he was fake, and her eyes were finally open. Pastor Prangles was quick to remind me that Momma walking away from the church equated to her walking away from God. It was a confusing time for all of us. I knew Momma was strong in her faith, but we were conditioned to believe that Pastor Prangles spoke for God himself. I didn't know God for myself. I only knew what Pastor Prangles told me.

That is the con of the small country church. The pastor presents himself as Lord over God's flock. He hovers over them, demanding attention like a spoiled child. And when that attention is not given, he throws a long-winded tantrum in the form of a sermon. That was the way of Pastor Rudders Prangles.

CHAPTER FOUR

I didn't leave when Momma left. Me and LJ stayed. There is an arrogance in small churches. An arrogance mixed with a cruel ideology. The belief that no other church is right or is teaching God's word correctly. LJ and I were essential members of the congregation; I was the devotional leader and he played the drums. We were a small congregation of thirty and somehow we thought that all of Heaven belonged to us...ONLY! Even though eight years had passed, I was still young and naive. I believed every word out of Prangles mouth. Pastor Prangles' cult-like ministry constantly reminded us that "No one teaches the truth like I am" or "If you leave this church you are gonna fall and everything you touch will fail."

Trueway Church was a stronghold of intimidation that trapped and misled the young, hurt, broken or lonely. Every member encompassed one of those features. My brother LJ and I embodied those characteristics. We were broken, searching for a father figure. Our desire to feel a father's love blinded us to the effects of that venomous ministry. Prangles knew that and he seized every opportunity to play on our self-doubts and insecurities. He gave us titles and jobs LJ played the drums and I was Deacon Terrell. I was the church trustee and Youth Sunday school teacher. I was also the pastor's armor bearer and scripture reader in church. Not only that, but I was the guy they called when he wanted to get the "Holy Ghost party" started.

I stood about 5'10" in height and was built like a Sumo wrestler. My midsection refused to stay above my belt line, spilling over into my lap. I had skin the color of soft brown leather and two dimples that pressed deep into my cheeks. Chestnut brown eyes and thick brows and lashes made my round face stand out. My self-esteem was low because of my weight but I didn't know it.

I was 18 when I met Tanya at Trueway church. She was the best singer in the choir. That made me feel important. I was filled with vanity and pride. Tanya was the first woman that showed real interest in me, and I latched onto her. She wasn't a gorgeous woman, but she had pretty features. Tanya was 5'4" with big, round brown eyes. Her voice and her apple ass were her greatest assets. She had small adolescent tits and a thick midsection that made her breasts seem even smaller. She was raised in the church...the old-school church. The kind that wore skirts below the knees. She had dark brown skin, a shade lighter than brown autumn leaves. She wore her hair in a French roll that made her look older than she was.

I was attracted to her because she was attracted to me. I had learned how to look like a Christian, talk like a Christian, and even dance like a Christian. I could hold a conversation with any minister and quote scriptures off the top of my head. I was never real about it. I enjoyed the attention and allowed it to change who I was. I had forgotten the core values that my mom had instilled in me. Pride, vanity and regular church girl pussy will do that to you.

My ego and my penis were the guiding forces in my decision to stay at Trueway Church. Momma's eyes were opened to the con of the Pastor, but I wasn't convinced. I listened to his ungodly bullshit. I listened to him say that Momma was weak. I even convinced myself that she was wrong for leaving. I knew my mother hadn't lost faith, but I was caught up in my new position in the church. I was young, naïve, and I was a Deacon.

Often in small churches, we equate titles to closeness with God. I was just plain stupid. I was the typical young adult with hormones. A few times those hormones got the best of me and that young, talented choir singer. She conceived a child, and in my distress and embarrassment to try and keep it hidden, I asked her to terminate the pregnancy. The frustration and stress of not wanting the church to know that we were sinners caused us both to agree that an abortion was the best solution. I had looked down my nose at so many folks, and now here I was covering up my own mess hoping not to be exposed. Tanya's conscience was heavy. She felt an urge to testify about her ordeal. She confessed to "our" sins in a long drawn out tearful soliloquy during testimony service.

In small churches in the south, there is a moment called testimony service. I always hated testimony service. I never understood how talking openly to sinners about their sins made them less sinful.

Church folk have a confusing habit when it comes to sharing testimonies. They tend to prefer telling dramatic stories about dark, reckless pasts turned around in a sudden moment just to grab the attention of the crowd and stir their emotions. Church folks are the best actors. They read the crowd, waiting for that climactic moment to tell of God pulling them up from the lowest moment.

"And that's when God stepped in right on time."

A swell of emotion brought other church folk to their feet, dancing and congratulating for believing in God and for telling your business to judgmental, gossiping ears and eyes. The more dramatic the story, the better.

At Trueway Church there seemed to be an obsession with sensational testimonies. There was a hunger for the juiciest story or gossip. This hunger was what propelled church folk to tell their stories, ending them with a "this changes everything" moment and "because I openly told you all my business, I'm all better." I have sat through hundreds of so called "testimony services" and said to myself, "Now you know that shit didn't happen like that" or "that negro knows he is lying."

I had to leave Trueway Church to understand that struggle is a reality. Temptation is a reality. Failure is a reality, even for those who are actively walking with Christ.

But that wasn't the way of Pastors Rudders Prangles. According to him, God was perfect, and we should be perfect. Anything less than perfection was ungodly. It was a hard life. No one can be mistake free. And after Tanya's confession, he latched hold to her testimony and in all self-righteous glory, proceeded to bring down condemnation on me as a sinner. He walked through the bible, twisting the scriptures to promote his own agenda of marriage and of filling his congregation.

"Adam *knew* Eve, and she did conceive. Genesis 4."

"King David *knew* Bathsheba, and she did conceive. II Samuel 11."

"And Deacon Terrell *knew* Tanya, so he must do the right thing."

I sat there Sunday after Sunday hearing the same thing over and over. I finally consented to marrying her. The church went through the same routine of shouting and jumping. I sat there, feeling that something was wrong. The pressure to do what this man said was overwhelming. The pressure to do what the Pastor said was an unbearable stronghold. My mind told me to flee, but my heart wouldn't allow me to. He assured me that I was doing what God wanted. He assured me that I was doing the will of The Almighty. He assured me that I would be blessed. And because of all these assurances, I followed his plan. On July 17, 1999, I married Tanya at the age of 24 off the word of my pastor.

CHAPTER FIVE

Almost immediately things went downhill. We initially moved in with her parents, in Denmark, South Carolina. It was degrading. We went to church Sunday after Sunday. Each Sunday, I was in the prayer line. I stood there in front of the Pastor.

"Young man, what are you asking God for?"

Each Sunday I would reply, "Pastor, me and my wife need a house."

Pastor Prangles presented himself as Lord over his congregation. Somehow, asking him to pray for you always felt like you were asking him to release your blessing. His presence made you feel as if he was the hand of God. So, we all waited for him to reach for the olive oil and recite his redundant prayer opening

"Father God in the name of Jesus."

Each Sunday, I would close my eyes and squeeze Tanya's hand tight. I wanted a house so bad. I wanted to feel like a man so bad. I wanted to feel some measure of success. So, I focused on every word the Pastor said. I believed him and believed in him.

"In Jesus name, we pray...Amen."

I would leave church filled with anticipation. I believed with all my heart that I would get a house...any house. I had worked hard in the church. I felt like somebody owed me something. I felt like I had the inside prayer line to God because I was the Pastor's right hand. As Deacon Terrell, my life was supposed to be spectacular. Every Sunday after prayer, a strong feeling of joy would overwhelm me. The church would begin clapping, the drummer would grab his sticks, the organist would tickle the keys, and the bass player would grab his guitar. We would dance all around that church. The entire church danced with us. Everybody was happy for us. Each Sunday, we went back to her parents' house with a renewed type of faith. This routine went on for months, and then one Monday I went to work and found a house to rent. I immediately called the Pastor.

"We're moving sir. God has blessed us," I cried with joy.

He asked, "Where is the house?"

"Sir, we are renting a little house in Blackville, South Carolina," I said.

He laughed. "That's good. Now that you're blessed, don't forget God."

His sentiment guised his real meaning. We had been blessed, now it was our turn to bless the church. Unusually that meant putting a little something extra on the plate.

"Oh, yes sir Pastor," I said. "I'm going to remember God, Sir."

We went to church that Sunday and danced again. It was the same pattern. Sunday after Sunday, shout, jump, dance, pay your money, then leave. Shout, jump, dance, pay your money, then leave. Sunday after Sunday. We had a form of Christianity based on a cult like ministry. Pastor Prangles was the new Jim Jones. He was another Charles Manson, instilling fear and condemnation in anyone that didn't praise God and thank HIM.

By the time Tanya and I moved into our new home, she was focused on someone else. She loved the spotlight of the church, but the routine and pattern was growing old to me. She wanted me to follow all the "prophecies" that I was going to be a minister. I couldn't see it. I wanted out of that fish bowl, but she didn't. So, she began confiding in Minister Lawrence. Lawrence was a young minister from another church. "On fire for the lord," but he was also on fire for my wife. Tanya didn't have a job, so while I was at work, Minister Lawrence was working on her.

CHAPTER SIX

About three years and three children into the marriage, Lawrence began showing up to church on a regular basis. He was a short, skinny guy who looked like Flava Flav in the face. The complete opposite of me. He was loud and flashy and always had a crease in his forehead from wearing his dew rag too tight. He wore the type of suits you would see in old gangster movies, the ones with the long overcoat and several buttons. He wore Steve Harvey suits before it became a trend.

I never liked Lawrence. His perfect waves and wing-tipped black and white Stacy Adams always bothered me. Here was this short, loud, pimple of a man who I felt was challenging me for my role in the church. It was a spot that I had worked for, a spot that I turned on my Momma for. Lawrence wasn't only there for my position in the church. He was there for the position in my house. Every visit coincided with money missing from our account and my wife mysteriously leaving late in the evenings. I was naïve and slightly stupid.

One evening, after a long church service I asked,

"Tanya, where are you going?"

She looked at me and said, "What do you mean, where I'm going?"

"I mean, it's six o'clock, and we have been to church since ten this morning. Now, you're

changing your clothes and going out to dinner. Where are you going?" I asked, anger obvious

in my voice.

"OUT, Terrell."

"Oh, I'm Terrell now," I uttered, contemptuous that she would forget my title. "I ain't deacon T."

"I don't know what you are."

"What the hell does that mean?"

"You ain't my daddy! That's my car and I ain't your slave."

I watched her storm out the door. This was the first of many slip outs, sisterhood meetings, missionary meetings, or emergency pastor's aide meetings, all taking place at night. These meetings all culminated with more and more money leaving our account. Tanya's leaving didn't bother me as much as the account being emptied. I was the only person working, so all the money was mine. She wasn't fiscally responsible. I had to allowance her a certain amount of money while still keeping the bills paid. This wasn't good enough for her, and one weekend while on a "Sisterhood" trip to North Carolina with Pastor Prangles' wife, she wrote checks from a checkbook she had stolen from me. Seven hundred dollars worth of bad checks written, just to impress the Pastor's wife. Seven hundred dollars worth of bad checks just to look good in front of the missionaries. And not one of them had the strength or character to correct her. When she came home from her religious trip, all the bills were due and the bank account was in the negative.

"Tanya, I got a call from the bank. They are saying a check bounced."

She looked me up and down and said, "Well, I don't know who is spending the money."

My teeth clenched as I asked,

"So, you didn't spend the money?"

She laughed.

"I don't need your money. I got my own money."

"WHAT MONEY!" I screamed. "Tanya, you don't work, you don't contribute to this house, you don't bring anything to the table. You don't cook, you don't clean, and as soon as I come home from work, I'm stuck with the kids while you go out on your church missions."

This was a constant fight. Money was always an issue. We were young. Neither of us knew how to save, but I *did* know how to pay my bills. She brought nothing to the table except bad sex,

a fertile womb, and debt. I slowly began to hate her.

I felt my rage building inside

when she said,

"Well, if you don't appreciate me then someone else will."

She wasn't just suggesting that there was someone else, she was telling me. I knew what she meant. I knew she had someone else. I could feel it. She was a liar, and a very poor one at that.

"What does that mean?" I asked.

She walked out the house, got in the car and left.

I immediately called the pastor.

"Sir, my wife—"

He stopped me mid-sentence.

"Son, I don't want to hear about your wife. She's a good girl, she's leading two songs this week for our choir, and we are going to sing off. Stay off her back."

"But, Sir," I uttered, trying to get a word in.

"Don't 'but Sir' me, Deacon Terrell. This is why you are not blessed," he shouted.

"Yes Sir. Alright, Sir. Whatever you say, Sir," were my only responses for the next thirty minutes.

I sat there for a while, questioning myself.

Was I overreacting? Could she really be doing the Lord's work, or was she doing the Lord's preacher? She came back around ten that night.

"Long night?" I said sarcastically.

"Don't start, Terrell," she huffed.

"Good night, Tanya."

She went into the bathroom and I heard the shower turn on. I laid there fuming. We went a few days without speaking. Sunday's sermon was about husbands who don't appreciate good wives. I sat there listening and looking around. I knew everybody was watching me. Every "Amen, Pastor" and "That's right, Pastor" was directed toward me. Lawrence was visiting and seemed to be particularly loud. Or maybe it was my imagination. I could feel anger growing inside me. We went home after church. I sat there quietly the entire ride home. I looked at that silly smirk on her face. We arrived home and her routine continued. She left, and I cooked for me and the kids.

The next day was November 13, 2001. I remember that day because when I went to work, we had a huge meeting about losing funding for our jobs. George Bush had ended the Welfare to Work grant that Bill Clinton initiated. I was a housing coordinator for this program. My job was to assist welfare mothers with finding homes and partnering with local community agencies to help them find employment. It was a rewarding job. I loved helping people get back on their feet, even though I was struggling.

Financially, Tanya and I were barely making it. Money, or a lack thereof, will ruin a relationship. We constantly argued over love offerings, special offerings and her secret donations to Pastor Rudders. I didn't realize until later how much I despised him. Why would he accept money from a struggling family? He had three cars. I had a 1985 grey Dodge Plymouth that I had to tip out of service twenty minutes early to avoid the embarrassment of everyone hearing me trying to start it. My bank account was bleeding money, hemorrhaging from Tanya's constant donations. We argued everyday over her "special sisterhood meetings," and when I found out my job was ending, the arguments became more intense.

I decided to leave work early that day and go home after the staff meeting. Just as I walked out the door, I saw a tow truck loading my car.

"What the hell are you doing?" I yelled.

The guy squatting down attaching my car to the lift didn't even turn around to look at me. He was an oversized white guy with tattoos covering his arms and neck. His round belly fell far over his beltline, and his breathing was heavy. No one was intimidating this guy and his nonchalant response to me confirmed that.

"Hey guy, we got an order to repossess this vehicle," he said with a strong southern twang.

"Man, I made my payments," I pleaded.

"Sir, it says right here you are three months behind. I just hook 'em and pull' em. Take that up at the office."

He handed me his clipboard to sign. I stood there looking stupid and feeling ashamed. All my coworkers stood around the windows. I could hear the giggling. I went back inside and listened to their half-ass attempts at consoling me.

"It will be okay."

I wanted to scream, "I don't want to hear that shit!"

But I was Deacon Terrell, and I learned that the perception of righteousness was just as important as being righteous. I had to maintain an image. So, I stayed calm, sat down, and called the bank. They informed me that I had several bounced checks on my account.

"But how?" I asked. "I haven't received any statements and I just got paid."

The teller explained,

"Sir, we have sent you several statements and there is also a warrant issued for all bounced checks over 500 dollars." I felt a chill race down my spine.

"Warrant?" I asked.

"Yes, Sir, a warrant," she said.

"But how? Why?" I asked, struggling to make sense of this dilemma.

"Sir, I'm looking at your account now. You have made several withdrawals, each one on

your payday. It appears that you have been taking money out and then writing checks."

Confused, I said,

"Ma'am, I have not been to the bank in weeks. I think someone is accessing my account and

stealing my money."

"Have you lost your ATM card?" she asked.

"No, Ma'am," I said.

"Have you lost your checkbook?" she inquired.

"No, Ma'am," I said, growing more and more frustrated.

"Then how could someone steal your money?"

Her sarcastic tone infuriated me. I knew it was a valid question. I just didn't want to hear it right then.

"Ma'am, I don't know. Is there any way to pull up the footage from the ATM?" I asked.

"Sure, Mr. Moorer. I can do that for you. Come this afternoon and I will have all of that laid

out."

Her tone was condescending. I knew she thought I was full of shit. It didn't matter to me.

I wanted to know where my money went. I thanked her and then hung up the phone. My next call was to the police station and sure enough there was a warrant. I called Tanya.

"Hey, they just repoed the car, and the bank is saying that the money is gone. We are almost 500 dollars in the negative"

My voice was frantic, and my heart raced waiting for her to help make sense of this situation. She was silent for several unnerving seconds and then she spoke...carefully.

I vigorously listened to her on the phone, my anger boiling inside. I listened to her lies and believed her. This was my wife and I so desperately wanted to believe her. I wanted to believe that something in my life wasn't fucked up. I wanted to believe that when the chips were down, Tanya had my back and that she wouldn't sabotage our house. After all, this is how we fed our kids. This is how we kept a roof over our heads. Why would she sabotage that? So, I believed her when everything in me said not to. I gave her the benefit of the doubt in my heart when my head said not to trust her.

"Terrell, I didn't touch the money. I didn't spend any of the money," she started.

I listened then asked,

"Tanya, I pay all of the bills and I know I didn't overspend. The police are looking for me and I don't have a ride."

She said,

"I'll get my parents car and I'll come get you."

"Come now please. I can't face these people at work."

About an hour later, Tanya drove up in her mom's white Honda Civic. I was already outside sitting on the steps. I was ashamed and embarrassed. I fought back tears of frustration as I walked over and got in on the passenger side of the car. I called my pastor from the car. The conversation with him infuriated me even more.

"Son, you tie God's hands when you don't live right," he said in his self-serving, self-righteous, funky ass tone.

I sat there on the phone with tears in my eyes. Every Sunday I had given my best and nothing was working out for me. I looked over at Tanya and asked her to go to the bank.

"Why?"

I told her that the bank manager had pulled up the video

of the person withdrawing the money from our account. To my surprise, she said, "Good."

I looked at her in amazement. "Really," I said.

"Yes, really, Terrell. I didn't take that money."

"Okay, Tanya. I believe you."

That one conversation had given me hope. I needed something. I was searching for anything to believe her, to believe that this marriage wasn't a complete sham, to believe that my life wasn't a cancerous pool of destruction. We drove down to the bank planning what we were going to say and who we were going to prosecute. It took us thirty minutes to get there. We spent the entire drive to the bank talking, planning and plotting. Every word out of her mouth gave me confidence. As bad as that day was going, the conversation in the car gave me faith. I felt like my wife was with me and I believed in her. For a brief moment, I felt like everything was going to be okay. We pulled into the bank parking lot and I dried my tears. I opened my door and stepped out of the car. Tanya never opened her door.

"What are you doing?" I asked, feeling confused.

"Terrell, I'm not going in there."

"Tanya, what the hell is going on?" I asked as I looked at her in disbelief.

Every bit of confidence I had in her vanished instantly. I felt a sinking feeling inside. I knew right away that she had taken the money. But I wasn't prepared for what I would see on the video. I walked in and introduced myself to the bank manager. She asked for my identification.

She apologized and said,

"You didn't look like the man in the video."

"Excuse me?" I asked. "What man?"

She said, "Come in and look at the video."

I sat in her office and watched the tape. My body went numb. I watched my wife and Minister Lawrence walk into the bank. I watched them pull up to the drive-thru teller, and I saw them taking my money. Taking my kids money. Here I was losing everything, and this woman was ripping me off. My body shook with rage. Murder filled my heart. I walked outside and got in the car.

The first thing she asked was "What did you see?"

"Bitch, you know what I saw."

I felt my body tense. For an instant, I looked in the mirror and saw my step dad. I felt his rage. I wanted to slap half her damn face off. I wanted to fuck her up bad! But I restrained myself. Seething with anger, I slammed my clenched fist against the car door over and over as my rage built. She was stealing from me, bringing me down. Hurting our family and lying. The thought of becoming my step dad haunted me. I wanted to slap her...but I refrained.

"Who are you cussing at, Deacon Terrell?" she asked.

This self-righteous BITCH was taunting me. She was trying to push my buttons.

"If you know what is good for you, Tanya, you will shut the hell up and just drive home."

It was a threat that I meant. We rode home in silence. She could feel my anger. My breathing was heavy, and my eyes watered with rage. I thought of all the things I could have done if I wasn't with her. I thought of all the places I could have been if I didn't tie myself down to her. My life would have been different. But it wasn't. And any thoughts of being somewhere else or doing other things was a dream, a fairytale, a figment of my imagination. I had to live in my reality. My reality was a lying, cheating, stealing, lowlife woman. My reality was that I was trapped in a situation that I no longer wanted to be in. My reality was a church that I hated as much as I hated my wife. I tied them together. They were inseparable. Each had slowly taken a piece of my life away from me. Each had slowly drained a little of my existence. I was dying inside. And when Tanya broke the deafening silence in the car, I was finished.

"Do you want to call the Pastor?"

"Prangles is your fucking pastor, not mine."

"Terrell, you need to pray."

"PRAY...Pray!" I screamed.

I sat there thinking about opening that door and pushing her silly ass out in the street. I thought about it the entire ride home. Job ending, car repossessed, wife cheating, money gone, and she was talking about praying. I had had enough praying. I had enough of the church, church folks, and of talking to her bullshit feeding pastor. None of it was working for me. I worked hard, and I did everything that preacher said would put me in "God's favor," and still nothing was working out for me.

I never envisioned my life like this. I was the devotional leader, the Sunday school teacher, the youth advisor and the church clerk. Why wasn't I blessed like Prangles said? Why wasn't my life moving in the direction Prangles said it would? Where was my car and my big house? The Pastor had one. Me and my wife were living with her parents AGAIN. She was pregnant AGAIN! And all Bishop Prangles could say was "Have faith." FUCK FAITH! His house was being remodeled while he was telling me to have faith. He was fixing up his house with my tithes and offerings, but my faith wasn't strong enough. I built my life off his words. I married this woman off his words. I lived in this fucked up town off his words. That was the con.

He didn't want to lose members. He didn't want to lose offerings, so he would tell us anything to make us stay. He accepted the credit for all the success and pointed the finger at the individual for any of the failures. I paid attention to the con. I paid attention to the manipulation. I made up my mind that things would change. Nobody gives a damn, so why should I? That night I walked outside. I looked up at the stars as I paced back and forth. I began to talk to myself out loud.

"This ain't right and I'm done! I tried. Where is my blessing? Where is my nice car? Where is my good job? Folks looking at me and laughing. Car got taken from my job."

I continued my rant, getting louder and louder.

"I'm sick of this shit. FUCK IT. FUCK ALL OF IT. FUCK THEM FAKE ASS

CHURCH FOLK...FUCK THIS WHOLE DAMN LIFESTYLE.

FUCK IT, FUCK IT, FUCK IT...IM DONE!"

Standing outside in the night air was my moment of clarity. It was my turning point. I felt like the world was against me. And in a sense, it was. Church was my world and none of it was the same. Church had become a lie to me. It was a place of corrupt dialogue and perversions. My world had changed. I was spoon fed a religious system that I believed in. I believed in faith, the preacher, tithing and the love offerings. I believed in it all and the system I believed in had let me down. I sat down on my front porch steps in the chilly night air. My breathing was hot and heavy causing steam to blow with each breath.

I thought to myself,

"Since everybody wants to piss on me, I'll piss back."

That's when I turned my attention to Yolanda.

CHAPTER SEVEN

T he thought of cheating on my wife had never crossed my mind. I was a devoted husband and God-fearing man. I wasn't in love with Tanya, but I did love her. I never wanted to do anything that resembled any action of my step dad.

Yolanda sang on the choir with Tanya. She was a friend of Tanya's but not a close friend. That is how I justified what I was about to do.

It all started innocently. Yolanda was a student at the local college. She was new to the area and new to the South. She constantly said that Southern men weren't her type, but I knew right away that she wanted attention. I wanted to rebel. I wanted to hurt some folks and I wanted satisfaction. So, I gave her what she wanted and lied to get what I wanted. I was still Deacon Terrell, so no one questioned me driving out to the college campus to "encourage" the college students. I took them all for a ride and sat there and talked to them about church and school. When everyone else left, I stayed around to pay a little extra attention to Yolanda.

"How's the college life?" I asked.

She always replied, "Life's good."

"You met a southern man yet?" I coyly asked.

"A southern man can't do anything for me," she replied.

Smiling, showing my deep dimples, I responded,

"You just haven't met the right southern man."

"Who's the right man? You?" she asked, her voice thick with a Brooklyn accent.

"I could be," I replied.

"But you're married."

"Marriage is what you make it." I shrugged.

"So, what are you trying to make of your marriage?" she asked.

"I'm trying to make it disappear," I laughed.

"Okay, and what are you trying to 'make' with me?" she asked.

"I'm trying to make you moan, scratch my back, bite my neck and maybe nibble on my

nipples. I like that shit," I said still smiling.

Yolanda wasn't prepared for my response. My use of profanity excited her. I was the church "bad boy" to her. This playful banter went on for weeks. I wasn't sure if she was interested, so I said what I wanted to say and played it off as a joke. I watched her reaction. I looked into her eyes and watched them dance when I flirted with her.

Yolanda was a heavy-set girl with a strong New York accent. Her skin was a shade darker than brown sugar and her hair touched her shoulders. She carried herself well and she had a very pretty face. Her self-esteem was low. All the females she associated with were thinner than her. She was beautiful, but she didn't know it. So, I showed her attention and ignored all of the other girls. She felt special. We played back and forth with many flirtatious conversations for a few months. The entire time we were feeling each other out.

I felt a renewed interest in church for the wrong reasons. It was the thought of having a secret. It was the thought of knowing that everyone was on the bandwagon, but I was finally off. Yolanda graduated from Denmark Technical school and moved to my hometown of Orangeburg to attend South Carolina State University. She wanted a four-year college degree in criminal justice. I loved her being in my hometown. It gave me an excuse to see her. My discontent for the church was so great that I didn't care who knew what I was doing. My hate made me reckless and when Yolanda asked me to help her move, I jumped at the opportunity. I called her and told her I was on my way.

I arrived on the campus of Denmark Tech and parked in the front of her dorm. On all of my other visits, I parked a distance away and walked to her room in the shadows.

Tonight, I didn't care. I walked through the dorm front door and knocked on her door. She opened the door with a smile.

"How did you get away from your wife?" she asked inquisitively.

"She's just my wife in name but you're my wife tonight," I said.

She smiled. She loved the attention, and I loved her smart mouth. She took my hand, fondling my wedding ring as she said,

"I'm not your wife. I'm not the one you go home to and I'm not the one you are sexing."

That was my opening.

"You couldn't handle it if I did."

She was quick with her retort,

"You don't know what I can handle."

I laughed,

"Little girl, I'm a grown man and I do grown man things."

"Grown man. All I see is a country boy," she said.

I loved her quick wit and fast responses. She could give it and take it. At that moment, I knew this was the night. The months of flirting would end this night. The anticipation would finally be answered. I helped her pack the items from her dorm room and drove her to Orangeburg.

Yolanda had found an apartment a few weeks before she started school. Her deposit was paid, and she had the key. This made her move seamless. I packed her belongings in my 1995 grey Dodge Plymouth and moved her into her little one-bedroom apartment. She didn't have much so I only needed to make one trip. It took a few hours to move her in completely. When we were done, I gave her a little hug.

She looked at me and asked, "Is that all I get?"

"What else do you want?" I asked.

She said, "You."

I took my jacket off and walked over to her. We kissed for the first time. She stepped back, pretending to resist and I followed her. I grabbed her and pulled her to me.

"If we are going to do this, then you can't leave me."

I looked her in the eyes and said,

"I won't leave."

She removed my shirt and I kissed her again. I held her close to me and she nervously shook. It had been a while for her. I lied and told her that I wasn't sleeping with my wife. She believed me. She thought I was deprived sexually, and she wanted to make up for it. She wanted to fix me and do the things that my wife didn't do. And she did. She slowly sucked on my neck and dragged her tongue down my chest.

I thought to myself,

"This is so wrong but feels so right."

She was aggressive. She pushed me on the bed and began to unbuckle my pants. I let her. She grabbed the bulge in the front of my pants and placed it between her lips. I closed my eyes in pleasure. She stayed there for a long time, sloppily embracing my erection with her mouth. My body tensed as she swallowed my full release. I couldn't believe what was happening. She sucked my soul out of me. It was the first time I ever had oral sex. She stroked my spit-soaked penis until I was stiff again. And then she climbed on top of me, placing me inside of her. She straddled my body and rotated her hips slowly. Her ample breast bounced up and down.

Our bodies moved uncoordinated at first and then we found a rhythm. I felt her body flinch as she released her orgasm. I rolled on top of her. It seemed like hours of pleasure. We both knew we were wrong but this wrong felt right and so good. Each stroke was me fucking the world. Each thrust was me saying fuck you Tanya. Each propulsive force was my way of regaining a little bit of myself. I exploded in exhaustion. My release was my freedom. As I laid next to her, my cell phone rang. It was two in the morning and I hadn't been home in hours. I didn't care. I fell asleep. I woke up to an unnerving feeling. I was comfortable. Too comfortable. I got up to leave.

"You promised to stay," she said.

"Yolanda, you know I can't stay," I replied.

She cried as I walked to my car and drove away. I had to turn my phone off because of the constant calls. When I got home, I didn't even look at Tanya nor did I answer her questions. She knew what I was doing. All women know when shit changes in the relationship. I knew she would tell the Pastor. Fuck it! Who cares. Nothing he said worked so what could he do? Preach at me? I didn't believe in him no more and nothing he said mattered to me. That night, I slept with a smile on my face. I could hear Tanya in the bathroom on the phone. She was talking to the First Lady Prangles, the Pastor's wife, telling her that I was out all night. Telling her she didn't know who I was with. I didn't care. I slept well. It was the beginning of my conscious leaving.

The next Sunday I was back in front of the church doing my Deacon thing. The Pastor came in and asked me to stop.

"I Timothy 5:8 says, 'A man that doesn't take care of his family is worse than an infidel and an infidel has no part with God,'" he yelled.

"Thou shalt not commit adultery," he continued. "You, Deacon Terrell, can't do anything in this church until you get right with God. Now sit in the back of the church."

Tanya was on tape with a minister stealing my money and *I'm* no good. I thought about all the money that my mom had given, I thought about all of the time I devoted, I thought about all of the long drives up and down the road for this counterfeit preacher. Sunday morning service, Sunday night service, Tuesday night bible study, Wednesday night prayer and business meetings Friday night, joy night service, and Saturday brotherhood meeting and choir practice. My whole damn week was spent in the church. But now I ain't no good.

"Okay, fuck it," I said under my breath. "I'll show you no good."

Yolanda saw my disappointment and she knew I would be going to her house that night. My attitude went from believer to "Fuck it!" That was my new motto.

"Fuck it!"

I left the church and went home to change my clothes. Tanya tried to talk to me, but I wasn't hearing anything she had to say.

She said, "You know you ain't living, right?"

I looked at her.

"I know your secrets, all of them."

"Do I need to remind you about your boyfriend, the bounced checks, and you giving that man my fucking money?"

I caught myself angrily walking towards her with my fists clenched. There were only two people I hated more than her, my step dad and Bishop Prangles. I wanted to make her feel my rage. I wanted to make them all feel my anger. I wanted to hit her, but I didn't...I couldn't. So, I went to Yolanda's house to work out my frustration on her vagina.

I entered her house as the aggressor. She was still in the dress that she wore to church. I pulled up the back of her dress and pulled down her panties. Bending her over the kitchen table, I penetrated her body. I stroked her until beads of sweat dripped from my forehead. She wanted to kiss me, but I didn't want to kiss. I wanted to use her body. I wanted to pound her vagina relentlessly. I wanted to make everyone feel my aggression. So, I used her over and over. Harder and harder. Grabbing her hips and pulling her against my erection. Pounding and pushing myself more aggressively with each stroke. Relentlessly and without affection. No feelings, no passion, just aggression. She loved me, and she was willing to be used just for my pleasure. My pleasure, my pain, my frustration and my anger were all I thought about. I didn't go home that night. I laid there thinking about leaving the church, my despicable wife and that fake ass Pastor. We woke early the next morning and didn't speak. I sat on the edge of the bed looking for my pants. I reached out with my foot and slid them over to put them on.

She rolled over and asked, "You leaving?"

My response was short. "Yes."

"You are going back to her?" she asked.

"I'm going home," I said, obviously agitated.

My responses were short, cold and emotionless. She knew I was married, and she knew what this was.

"How can you go back to her after last night?" she asked with tears in her eyes.

"Yolanda, you already know what this is and who I am. Last night was last night and today

is today. What the fuck you think I'm gonna do, move in with you?"

My response was harsh. I wanted it to be. I wasn't in love with her or my wife and I didn't

care. I wasn't leaving my wife for her and she knew it.

"What does that mean?" she asked with a quivering voice.

I wasn't exactly sure what I meant. So, I ignored her. Living with a nagging wife helped me perfect my ability to tune someone out. I could watch TV in the midst of the worst argument. All I knew was that the fantasy was over. It was a new day and I had to snap back to reality. I was that guy, that deacon, the married man, the father again. I stood up and buttoned my shirt. I walked out without speaking. I wasn't really interested in talking to her. She had feelings, I didn't. She was in love, I wasn't. I took the long drive back to Blackville. Tanya was there packing her clothes when I walked through the door.

Surprised, I asked, "Are you leaving?"

She didn't say anything. Knowing that she was ignoring me didn't faze me at all. I loudly said

"Who the fuck cares" as I walked into the bedroom to wash Yolanda off of me.

"Terrell, you a cold-hearted bastard. You're gonna to get yours, you just watch. God doesn't

like what you are doing, and you are going to get yours."

I stood there in the bathroom doorway amazed. Even now she was continuing her hypocritical front. Everything in me said, "Avoid this conversation," but I couldn't. I loathed her, and I wanted her to know.

"Did you just say God doesn't like what I am doing? Did you just say, 'God is going to get me?'" I asked in a rage.

An uncontrollable laugh came over me. This bitch was clueless. Who the fuck cheats and

then pretends to be the victim. It was time. It was time to have this conversation. It was time to let everything off my chest. I took a deep breath, walked back to the room she was in, looked her in the eye and said,

"FUCK YOU, TANYA. FUCK YOU, YOU thieving, lying, no good bitch! Fuck you, fuck your church, fuck your pastor, fuck your feelings and fuck your boyfriend! I SAW you at the bank. I saw you in the photos and the videos. I should have fucked you up on site, but I chilled and let it ride. YOU STOLE FROM ME! YOU STOLE FROM YOUR CHILDREN! My car was taken...repo-ed. NOT YOURS! You put our whole family in jeopardy. You cost me EVERYTHING. You are a pathetic, disgusting, bitch of a woman. And I hate you. I swear to God, I hate you. I wish I could erase you. I wish I could erase the day that I met you. I wish I could go back and talk to that guy and tell him you are a fucked up, broken ass woman. I wish I could go back and tell him you are a fake ass cheating bitch that can't fuck or suck a dick."

Her tears didn't faze me. The venomous words continued to spew from my soul. I saw

her tears race down her cheeks as I launched a slew of attacks, criticizing her body, her cooking, her conduct, her house keeping. Everything! She was stealing, lying and cheating for months, maybe even years, and God was going to "get me!" She had been following that pastor and jumping around that church all these years and God was going to get me. Neither of us was right, I just decided to stop being a hypocrite. I decided to stop playing.

In my eyes, I was better than them all. I finally stopped lying to myself. I finally was calling a spade a spade and a phony a phony. After my 45-minute diatribe of harsh words, I went to take a shower. After the shower, I laid down in the bed, unfazed at all about her leaving. I wasn't fully asleep when I felt her presence in the room. I knew I had said some ugly things and a part of me wanted to apologize. She wasn't a good person, but she was the mother of my kids. My compassion caused me to turn over. My love for her made me apologetic.

I sat up on the bed and said,

"Tanya, I shouldn't have spoken to you that way. I'm sorry."

There was a long pause after my apology. I thought to myself, "Maybe she doesn't want to talk." I laid back down and closed my eyes as Tanya left the room. As I drifted off to sleep, the room door flew open.

Tanya was in a fury screaming,

"Who's sucking your dick? Who the HELL is sucking your dick?"

I sat up. I could see the anger in her eyes. Her anger made me angry. And I responded with the same energy she was emitting.

"You mean to tell me that out of that entire conversation THE ONLY THING YOU HEARD ME SAY WAS I GOT MY DICK SUCKED. FUCK YOU TANYA."

"No, fuck you, Terrell, and that fat bitch Yolanda," she

screamed. Her spontaneous revelation didn't disturb me at all. I didn't care if she knew. I didn't care who knew. I ignored her, rolled over and smiled as I closed my eyes.

I woke the next morning to the sound of pots clanging in the kitchen. I sat on the side of the bed listening to her angry cooking. Fearful and unsure if I wanted to eat what she had cooked, I avoided the kitchen. She walked past me as I sat on the couch.

"I thought you were leaving?" I asked.

She didn't say anything. I flipped the channel a few times and heard a knock at the door. It was her father and brother.

I extended my hand and asked,

"How you are doing, Mr. Tyler?"

He brushed past me and said,

"Sit down, son, we need to talk."

"Yes, Sir." I was always respectful.

"My daughter said you put your hands on her," he said with frustration in his voice.

"That's a damn lie, Sir," I said.

"Don't cuss at me, son," he said.

I watched as her older brother stood in the corner, clenching his fist. My patience was wearing thin as I sat and listened to her father. I watched her brother trying to punk me with menacing looks.

Her dad continued,

"If you didn't want my daughter, you shouldn't have taken her out of my house. I didn't give you my daughter to have you beat up on her. The bible says, 'Blessed is the man that

finds a wife,'" he said in an authoritative voice.

I could take it no more. I stopped him mid-sentence.

"Sir, it says that a man that finds a good wife is blessed. Your daughter ain't a good

wife, and if you want her back then take her," I said sarcastically.

As Tanya walked out of the room, I yelled,

"Leave if you want. I'm done with your lying ass."

She screamed,

"I'm not a liar. I'm leaving and I'm taking the children."

I responded, "So what, take your silly ass and get the fuck out. I don't give a shit. I'll get visitation after the divorce."

Her brother moved from the corner to the side of the couch. I was ready. I felt it coming and I was ready. I turned to him.

"What the fuck you gonna do?" I asked, waiting for the confrontation.

Ed, Tanya's brother, was not a small guy at all. He was known as "big country." Dumb as a box of rocks. He always had a blank look on his face as if it hurt him to think too much. He was used to working outside and had a country physique. The kind of body you would see on a slave. The kind of body you get from working in the field or cutting wood all day in the sun. He was about 6'3" and I was 5'10". I stood there, looking up at him with both fists clenched tight.

It wasn't the fight I would have picked for myself, but my mouth had played my cards and I was all in.

He looked down at me and spoke in his slow southern, hillbilly, country drawl,

"You ain't gone cuss my sister no mo!"

I was quick to respond,

"This my house, nigga. Fuck you and yo raggedy ass sister...you country, backwoods ass

mother fucker."

I got four brothers and one step brother. That's six boys. I could talk trash like a champ. Luckily for me, her father stepped in and sent Ed outside. I was relieved, but I didn't let them know it. I was two minutes from getting my ass whipped but I still talked like I was Mike Tyson. Tanya walked back into the room and I sat on the couch. Her father continued to talk as she packed her small bag. I didn't hear a word he said. She walked out carrying the children. I called Yolanda and told her I was coming over.

I drove to Orangeburg with my car packed. My intentions were to start over. I knocked on Yolanda's door. She opened the door in her panties and grabbed my belt buckle. She knew I was finally free, and she wanted me to be with her. She felt like we made love, but it was just slow sex. It wasn't one of my finest sexual moments but I knew I needed a place to stay and she needed to feel special. I put a few clothes in her closet. For the next few days, we rode around town like a new couple. She was excited, but the thought of being in a relationship sickened me. I didn't want to experience day after day of the same sex over and over again. She seemed to be in competition with Tanya. Every day was some stupid question about Tanya.

"Does Tanya do this for you? Does she kiss you like this? Does she touch you like this? Does she cook like this? Does she make you feel like this?"

I wanted to scream "Shut the fuck up and just keep sucking my dick."

Every day, her need to secretly compete with my soon to be ex-wife was annoying me more and more. I wanted to forget that chick. I wanted to forget that I had ever married her. Thinking about her only condemned me. Thinking about her caused my conscience to kick in and I didn't want to be conscientious of my actions. A few weeks went by. I stopped going to the church, but Yolanda didn't. And one Sunday afternoon, Yolanda came home from church with red eyes from crying, I could tell something was wrong.

I looked at her face and asked,

"What's wrong?"

She burst into tears and said, "I love you, but you're not mine."

"What do you mean, I'm not yours?" I asked.

The question was a formality because I knew the answer already. I was well versed in the sermons of Bishop Rudders Prangles. He had many sermons that evoked fear. He was a pro at making God a monstrous being who was at his beck and call, ready to reign down destruction on anyone Prangles thought was ungodly. He could stir fear into the strongest person with his "You're going to hell" sermons. His loud, thunderous voice would boom as he berated you with "You are a harlot, adulterer or a sinner and not a saint" sermon. Each one always ending with "Come to Jesus, just now, or you might not make it through the night."

Terror would consume you. The thought of God coming back to rapture his children and leaving you to die and burn in eternal hell fire was enough to make anyone bow down at the altar and beg forgiveness for his or her sins. I had seen this many times before. He would come in dressed in his black robe. The choir would sing and work the church into a frenzy. He would then stand up over the pulpit as the church grew quiet. In the background, someone would speak in tongues as he instructed the church to let the Lord speak.

"God is not pleased with what's going on in his house."

His authoritative voice would boom through the microphone as he instructed the church in "God's Word." He would spout thunderous words.

"In the last day, God shall separate the wheat from the tares, the good from the bad, the

righteous from the unrighteous. NO unrighteous shall see God."

It was his patent sermon of clichés. "Only what you do for Christ will last. God is the same yesterday, today, and forever more. Stand for God or you'll fall for anything."

And then there was the one he used when someone left the congregation. The parable of how Satan got cast out of heaven. I could tell by the fear on Yolanda's face that was the one. He could scare you into repentance with his rendition of the scripture.

I could almost hear him say in his southern preacher voice,

"Satan was a beautiful angel. And he lived in heaven with God. But Satan didn't want to conform to the ways of Christ. He wanted to take over heaven. God sent Michael to cast Satan out of his kingdom and the bible says that as Satan was cast out, he reached his tail back into heaven and dragged out a third of its angels. Now we sit here in this congregation and Deacon Terrell has left, and as he left, he reached back and is trying to drag our sister, but we ain't gonna to let him."

I imagined the men getting louder with their "Amens" and "You preaching, Pastor."

I could see Yolanda sitting in the pew as the cat calls from the Amen corner grew louder and louder. I knew the feeling she was feeling very well. I had experienced the judgmental eyes of that sacrilegious Pastor looking down on me. I knew how it felt to be in a church full of people and to feel alone. That feeling of knowing that everyone is looking at you and talking about you without saying your name directly. The feeling of being under the microscope and exposed. It's a naked feeling. A feeling of shame. I imagined Tanya crying and purging at the altar saying she wanted her husband back.

Putting on just enough of a show to build a thick cloud of compassion from the members.

And just when the air became suffocating with "Amen," crying and the sounds of missionaries speaking in tongues, that old southern preacher would come down with that bottle of olive oil, stand over her and ask,

"Daughter, can I pray for you?"

No one ever said no.

"Father God in the name of Jesus."

I can hear him telling God to save his lost daughter, forgive his lost daughter, send his prodigal daughter home. Give her strength to resist the devil. Don't let Satan pull her...

"In Jesus' name, we pray. Now give God some praise for the victory."

The church would then get worked up into a praise frenzy, shouting and dancing. I looked at Yolanda. She didn't have to tell me anything. I told her I would move out. I was somewhat happy. I wanted to leave but wasn't sure how. This way, I seemed like I really cared. I put the few clothes that I had at her house in my car and drove to my mother's. I hated all of them fucking frauds. As I drove out her yard, I turned the radio on and heard a soothing voice announcing songs. Her name was Ann Marie.

CHAPTER EIGHT

A nn Marie was a local radio announcer in a neighboring town. The station was about a 40-minute drive from where I lived. She was an older girl and very lonely. I knew the instant that I heard her voice over the radio I wanted to meet her. I called in to the radio station to request a song. She intentionally prolonged our conversation on the phone. I had only slept with Yolanda after Tanya and I separated, but it was getting old. It had been six months of the same old pussy, and I wanted to experience something new. My morals were rapidly declining and my thrust to fulfill my lusts increased. I was slowly becoming the same con artist that I loathed in Prangles. Using the scriptures and God to get what I wanted. Masking my words as words of care and concern, knowing that everything I said to Ann Marie was bullshit. Ann Marie was new to me.

The excitement of experiencing someone new intrigued me. I was feeling myself. I made small talk at first, quoting scriptures and talking about the goodness of the Lord. Pastor Prangles' clichés came in handy as I quoted some of them to her surprise. Minutes would turn into hours as we talked between her spinning records and plugging commercials. She was impressed with my knowledge of gospel music. I had been in the church my entire life. Ann Marie was a DJ at a gospel music station. She had a soft voice when answering the phone. I'm not sure if it was the late-night hour, but it was inviting.

"You're listening to WKKI all gospel all the time. My name is Ann Marie and I'll be with you until the morning hours."

"Hi, Ann. I'm Terrell. Can I hear something by Commissioned?"

"Commissioned is my favorite group," she said.

"Mine too," I said with glee in my voice.

"Really?" she said.

"Yes, I have been a fan since Fred Hammond was in the group," I replied.

"Are you going to the concert?" she asked.

"The reunion tour, of course," I asked.

"I'll be there, too," she said.

Something sparked in me at that moment.

"Hopefully I'll see you there," she paused.

"Maybe you will," I said slyly.

I could hear her smile over the phone.

"Maybe we could meet for lunch and talk?"

Before I could finish my question, she said, "Yes."

Desperation is unattractive in a woman, but for a predator it's sexy as hell. She was desperate and needy. A lot of older single church women are. We exchanged phone numbers off the air on a private line. I called her a few more times. She told me everything. She had never been married, but she loved the Lord. She didn't have any kids, but she loved the Lord. She was a virgin. She was active in the church...My mind went numb on the rest of our conversation. My attention was focused on her untouched vagina.

How could it be? How could it be untouched for so many years? Was that even possible? I had made up my mind. I was going to be her first. I really didn't care about anything else at that moment. I knew that the only thing that would open her legs was wedding bells. So, I focused on making her think I wanted what she wanted. I was getting good at lying. I was getting good at selling a story. I learned it from Prangles. I didn't realize it, but I was acting just like him. He was a spiritual whore, fucking members out of their hard-earned money. I, on the other hand, was a regular man whore. Months passed. Ann Marie and I talked every night I wasn't with Yolanda. After two months of anticipation, phone conversations, and flirting, Ann Marie and I agreed to meet.

I woke up early on a Saturday morning. I was excited about the possibility of meeting Ann Marie for the first time. I had told her that my car was in the shop and that I had to borrow a friend's car. I went over to Yolanda's house and told her I was going to wash her car for her. Yolanda always kept a full tank of gas and I was still unemployed. She was happy for any attention from me. I hadn't touched her in a few weeks and I hadn't been back to the church at all. When she saw me, she greeted me with a huge kiss and asked if I had a few minutes. I told her I was in a rush and I just wanted to wash her car. I was on the time table. I had a 45-minute drive to Columbia, South Carolina to meet Ann at 1 o'clock.

Yolanda pulled me into her house and unbuckled my pants. I couldn't say no. She knelt in front of me and placed my tip in between her tongue and the roof of her mouth. Slowly, she tickled the edges of my thick firm head circling my erection with her tongue. I leaned back against the wall as she sucked me completely inside her mouth. In and out, gently sucking while holding my testicles firm in her hand. My toes curled as she slid her tongue along my shaft, swallowing my testicles into her mouth. I opened my eyes to look down at my watch, but I couldn't bring myself to stop her. She spread my legs and slowly dragged her tongue to that spot above my asshole. I could feel her tongue enter me while her hands stroked my erect penis. Her soft hands moved over my swollen cock, spreading her spit up and down my shaft. She could feel my body tense as I was ready to climax. She knelt in front of me anticipating my release. I felt her mouth clamp down on my head, sucking harder. As she stroked my shaft with her hands, I exploded in her mouth. She continued to suck until there was nothing left. My legs went numb.

"Damn girl, what was that?" I asked.

She smiled. "You miss your little slut?"

"Hell yeah," I said.

"When you finish washing my car, I got something else for you," she said.

I looked down at my watch thinking, "The hell with Ann Marie."

I wanted to stay and fuck Yolanda, but the thought of Ann Marie's undefiled vagina got the best of me. I mean after all, Yolanda's pussy was effortless. I could get it at any time. I gave her a hug and borrowed 20 dollars from her. I told her I would be right back and left out. I didn't have time to wash off but since we didn't have sex, I still felt clean.

I called Ann Marie and told her I was running late. I asked her if she could meet me halfway. We agreed that Denny's was the halfway point. I pulled up at the restaurant and waited in the parking lot. Until that day, I had only heard her voice on the radio. I had never seen her in person. She described herself as 5'3" and petite. I looked around and spotted her immediately.

My first impression was "there is no way she's a virgin." She wore a skirt that rose up her thighs as she walked. Her skin was light brown, the color of a cappuccino. My eyes gazed at her perky firm breasts that seemed to be too large for her frame. Her thick hips and thighs pushed through the sides of her plaid pencil skirt, giving her body an appealing silhouette. Her hair was in curls and touched her shoulders. She wore red lipstick on her tightly pressed lips. She looked nervous...maybe even scared. It had been a long time since a man took interest in her. It had been a long time since she felt wanted. I looked at this attractive woman thinking "damn I'm going to get this."

Restraining myself was a chore. I wanted her instantly and I think she knew it. When she walked up, I greeted her with the "church" hug. My ass pooched out, careful not to let my pelvis touch hers. We exchanged greetings as I held the door open for her. As the waitress walked us to our seat, I watched her ass and thick thighs sway back and forth, taunting me. Daring me to reach out and touch them. Restraint was hard and so was the member in my pants. We sat down and ordered. I made small talk until our meals came. Unconsciously, I reached for her hand and prayed for the both of us. A part of me felt a little ashamed. It felt like I was using the church to manipulate this woman...but the thought of that unbroken hymen got the best of me.

She lifted her head and said,

"Wow, I'm impressed you prayed."

"I always pray over my food," I said proudly.

I responded with confidence, allowing her to know this was normal behavior. She loved the fact that I took charge. It made her feel like a wife with her husband in control. It was typical church girl behavior. We talked about everything:

school work, church, our families...everything. She laughed. I could tell it had been a long time since she laughed. I reached out and touched her hand. We talked some more and finished our meals. The subject of her virginity never came up. I didn't want to seem obsessed or even interested in it. But I was...the more she talked, the more I thought about it.

I imagined her laughter as my tongue tickled her nipples. I pictured her mouth opening wide and her eyes closing as I penetrated her for the first time. I was aroused at the table. We finished our food and I used Yolanda's twenty dollars to pay for our meal. When it was time to leave, I stood and gave her a hug, the church hug again. I knew that soon there would be no more church hugs. Soon our hugs would be full frontal touching. I reached down and grabbed her hand as I walked her out to her car. I opened her door and kissed her on the forehead. She smiled again. She had to tiptoe to kiss my cheek. It was electric. I felt myself tingle. I felt my pants move. I walked over to Yolanda's car.

I found a mechanical car wash and drove through it. I floored it back to Yolanda's house. My mind was consumed with Ann Marie: her smell, her hair, those thick thighs and that untouched vagina. As I thought about Ann Marie, I worked myself into a state of uncontrolled excitement and when Yolanda opened the door, I was the aggressor. I leaned in and kissed her. I grabbed her, walking her backwards toward the room, undressing her as we walked. I pulled her panties down, turned her around, and pushed her onto the bed. I grabbed her hips and pushed myself inside her. I flipped her over. I wanted to see her expression as I placed my hands on the back of her thighs, bending her legs, pressing her knees against her breast. I was inside Yolanda but thinking of Ann Marie. I closed my eyes and imagined her closed vagina spreading open for me. In my mind, I screamed her name while looking down at Yolanda. It was great sex. I rolled over and laid down on the bed. Yolanda leaned over and kissed me.

"What was that!" she asked with excitement. "You must have really missed me

I knew what she wanted to hear, so I lied.

"Yes, I missed you. I missed every inch of you," I said shamefully.

The lies came easier now. They were effortless. Yolanda went into the kitchen and cooked while I napped. I awoke to the smell of fried chicken and macaroni. Yolanda always cooked when she was happy, and I had just made her ecstatic. She came into the room with a plate.

"You hungry?" she asked.

"Yes, I am," I said.

"Good. I made your favorite. You earned it," she smiled.

I thought to myself, "Damn right I did."

After dinner, I laid in her bed until an hour before Ann Marie's shift started at the radio station, then I left.

This was a variation of my routine for the past few

months. I went to Yolanda's, stayed all day and went home to call Ann Marie.

"You're listening to WKKI all gospel all the time. My name is Ann Marie and I'll be with you until the morning hours." I loved her radio voice.

"Hi, Ann Marie, this is Terrell." I could hear the change in her voice every time I called.

"I knew you were going to call," she said.

I smiled and said, "I was thinking about you all day."

Her voice couldn't hide her excitement.

"I was thinking about you too, Terrell. Call me back on my cell phone."

I waited a few minutes. I had learned to call during the songs and not the commercial breaks. The DJ's program the songs during the commercial breaks. I dialed her number. She picked up on the first ring.

"Hi, Ann."

"Hi, Terrell."

She asked why I was up so late.

"I needed to hear your voice," I told her.

She told me that she had prayed for us. I was silent. I had limits to my hypocrisy.

"I want to see you again, Terrell, but I have to be careful," she said.

"Why?" I asked.

"Because I catch feelings really fast. And I don't want to be hurt."

"When can we have dinner Ann?" I asked.

"I don't know, Terrell. I don't want to rush things, and I don't want to get hurt."

I knew there was a story behind her fear of getting hurt. Her story was my opening. I wanted to hear it. I asked her again,

"We can go to dinner or I can cook for you?"

"Cook?" She seemed impressed again. "You can cook?" she asked.

I laughed and told her how many brothers I had.

"Of course, I can cook."

She paused and said, "Why don't I cook for you first?" The anticipation of me and her finally being alone excited me.

"Tell me when. I'm free all week," she said.

"How about Thursday night?"

"Sure."

We talked for a little longer, then I let her go. I laid down thinking four weeks of phone conversations was finally about to pay off. I closed my eyes.

Yolanda came to my mother's house early the next morning. I forgot I had asked her to take me job hunting. When I got up, she was downstairs talking to my mom. I remember thinking "I'm sick of this chick saddling up to my mom, it's time to move on," but I needed her car...so I tolerated her. We left the house together. I sat silently in her car.

"What's wrong with you?" she asked.

"Nothing," I said.

"Then why you so quiet?"

I looked at her and said, "No reason." We both sat quietly as she drove to a few companies in the area. I filled out two or three applications and was done for the day.

She asked, "Do you want to come over?"

I was sick of screwing her by now.

"Not really."

It had been months. The excitement, the mystery and anticipation were gone. It was difficult to get erect without imagining someone else. I was tired of her sex, but I needed to use her car. So, I went to her house. Yolanda liked to be comfortable. She always undressed as soon as she entered her house. She laid on the bed wearing only an old red t-shirt of mine, her feet flat on the bed with her knees bent just enough to put her beautiful, well-shaved vagina on display. She didn't pay any attention to me as I walked in and out the room, checking my phone to see if Ann texted. Yolanda was too wrapped up in Facebook and texting on her phone.

I remember thinking, "It's funny how the things that were once cute can make you sick when you want to leave." I found flaws in everything. Her gaping wide legs exposing her vagina once was sexy. Now it was just the desperate act of a hopeless woman trying to hold on to a connection that no longer existed. Reluctantly, I crawled onto the bed, sliding between her legs up towards her chest. I laid my head on her breasts. I could hear her heartbeat increase. All we had was sex. Nothing else. Our lives would never be anything else. I knew that telling her that would crush her. She was in love...and I was her first love. I didn't know what love was. The thought of it was tainted by my step dad and Tanya. Love was a unicorn. An imaginary creature that only existed in children's stories. She looked down at me as I looked up at her. She smiled. It was a smile of delight. She adjusted her body so that it settled perfectly under mine.

My hands slid smoothly over her thighs, appreciating how soft her legs were. She was very meticulous when it came to body maintenance. She shaved regularly and only used the finest of lotions. Her smell aroused me. I placed my hands under her red t-shirt, gently tracing along the lines of her hip bone. She inhaled deeply, and I could feel her muscles moving as my fingers explored her. She exhaled with a content sigh, urging me to continue.

I remember playfully asking, "Can I touch you here?" as my fingers teased her body. I knew the answers to my question. My innocent touches always turned her on. She liked when I asked for permission to run my hands up the sides of her breasts or to circle my thumbs softly over the tips of her nipples. The way she arched her back while slightly biting her lip was my indication that she was ready for anything I wanted. She moved her hips, spreading her legs wider, giving me more access to her freshly shaven honey pot. She relaxed her legs underneath me. That was my yes. It was her way of granting me access to her goodies as she continued typing away on her phone. I squeezed her clit between my forefinger and thumb, gently massaging her as she shifted her body. Her constant sighs and moans aroused me, coaxing me to move my hands between her warm, wet inner thighs. I happily took up the job of stimulating her. I passed two fingers up and down her slit, gently stroking her sensitive flesh while my thumb rubbed her clit. All the while, I watched her expression, delighting in the huge smile on her face. I soon felt her growing damp and allowed my fingers to graze a little deeper as they continued stroking back and forth. She released a deep moan as I pressed my thumb onto her clit a little harder and tentatively dipped one finger inside her.

A smile came to my lips when I find her dripping wet enough to really play. Keeping pressure on her clit, I slowly push two fingers into her and drag them back out. Her gaze is still fixed on her phone, but her eyelids flutter the slightest bit and she groans, arching her back as I push my fingers back in. I start a steady rhythm of massaging her clit and pumping my fingers, and the heat between her legs grows in intensity. She rolls her hips into my touch, grinding on my fingers and eventuall I notice her dragging her lower lip between her teeth. She puts her phone down on the nightstand and grabs the edges of the bed.

"You're so good at that," she coos, her voice absolutely dripping with sex. I smile and continue my steady movements, content just to watch her sigh and roll her hips against my hand. I use my free hand to push the hem of the old t-shirt up, exposing her perfect breasts and hardened nipples. She inhales and exhales like the flow of the tide, and I was determined to see a wave crash.

Her mind was perfectly in tune with mine as always. She gazed up at me with her eyes half opened. She reached her hand out, caressing my cheek while her thumb danced along my lower lip.

"Think you can finish me?" she asked, and even if I wasn't already wanting to do exactly that, the way she was watching me in that moment would have been enough to convince me anyway. She closed her eyes with a pleasured sigh as I pressed my thumb down on her clit again. I use that fleeting freedom from her entrancing gaze to back away from her, moving my body down the bed so that I can put my head between her legs. I revel in the way she sucks in a deep breath and holds it, her own anticipation building as she grips my bald head. The way her fingernails graze my scalp sends tiny sparks through every nerve in my body and I sigh, cascading hot breath over her. I briefly catch sight of her biting down on her lower lip before she gently pulls me into her.

I started with the very tip of my tongue, just letting it tease her lips, and I slowed my fingers to a stop so as to ensure she focused on what I was doing with my mouth. Her breathing was shallow, short, and controlled as I just barely flicked my tongue around—but not on—her clit. And I kept doing exactly that— only that—until she was just starting to squirm, her fingers on my bald head started to tighten their grip. That's exactly where I want her—right in the height of that tension—when I lay my tongue flat against her, dragging it all the way up from her entrance to her clit and finally closing my mouth around her and sucking.

I roll my fingers just so inside her, hitting that perfect spot at the same time that I suck on her clit once more, and she thrusts her hips up into me with one last definitive cry of release. She holds me in place as she rides out her orgasm, and I know to keep my tongue and fingers pressed firmly against her sweet spots until she's done. Finally, as she exhales a breath she was holding in, all the tension falls from her body and she releases me from her hold. I go to work with my tongue, making sure to clean up as she lays still and catches her breath, her small sighs encouraging me. Her chest is still heaving when she cups my face in her hands, dragging me up toward her. "Come here," she murmurs. "I want to taste myself on you." I happily obey, moving up her body to finally settle against her perfect, soft form. She greets my lips with hers, mouth open and waiting to meet my tongue half way. Our kiss is salty and sweet and hot, and she sighs in pleasure as she drinks it in.

"You're so good," she whispers as our lips part. "Would you like a turn now?"

I hum as if considering it.

"Nah, I just want to please you," I said.

"Are you sure?" she asked.

"Yes, I'm a little tired," I whispered, briefly lifting my head so I can pull my old t-shirt down over her body again. It compliments her form so much better than it ever did mine. I wouldn't complain if she wore that shirt for the rest of her life. She sighs, hugging me to her chest. The room is silent. I break the silence.

"Can I borrow your car Thursday night?" She was still in love and she worked nights. She agreed to let me drop her off and keep her car.

Thursday night came, and I could hardly contain my excitement. I drove Yolanda to her job and dropped her off. She kissed me goodnight. I laughed as I drove off and dialed Ann Marie's number.

"Hi, Ann."

"Hi, Terrell."

My heart was pounding with anticipation.

"Are we still on for tonight?" she asked.

"Yes, we are," I said.

I asked her for directions and then told her I was on my way. Yolanda was a corrections officer. She worked at the prison in Columbia, South Carolina. It was just my luck that Ann Marie also lived in Columbia. She lived about ten mins from Yolanda's job. I arrived at her place and knocked on the door. She came to the door dressed in a fitted jean skirt that showed her figure. She was beautiful, small waist, curvaceous hips and ample breasts. I gave her a hug as I walked through the door. Not the church hug. I leaned in and let her feel my excitement. It startled her a little, but I could tell she was impressed.

We walked over to her couch and she offered me something to drink. The house smelled of roast and potatoes. She had been cooking for hours but she pretended that she had just thrown something together. I sat on the couch and she sat next to me. After a little small talk about our families, she asked if I was hungry. I followed her into the kitchen, casually checking out her body. We sat down at the dinner table and I prayed over the food. I left the table with a full stomach. She joined me on the couch to watch TV. We innocently touched hands. I knew that I needed to take this slow and steady. Any perception of wanting more than to hold her hand would certainly turn her off. I rubbed my index finger gently over her fingers, lightly stroking her hand and wrist. She slid closer to me and I grabbed her whole hand. She began to run her hand up and down my arm. I couldn't contain my excitement. I leaned over and kissed her softly on the lips. She blushed a little and pulled back. I apologized immediately,

"I'm sorry," I said.

"For what?" she asked.

"I don't want to pressure you," I said.

She looked into my eyes and said, "I enjoyed it. I haven't been kissed in a long time."

I leaned in and kissed her again. This time she kissed

back. I felt her letting herself go. I felt her hands and her body giving in to me, so I stopped. I pulled back.

"Ann, we can't do this. I don't want you to think I'm just after one thing," I said, trying to sound like I gave a damn.

I saw the tears swell in her eyes. Her heart was full. She had finally met someone that wanted her and not just her body...she thought. She began to tell me about her ex.

"Terry was my old boyfriend. He kept pressuring me to have sex," she said with a quivering voice.

I listened attentively. She told me how he belittled her and how many times he cheated. She told me that he made her feel like it was her fault.

"He never wanted me, he just wanted my body. I loved him, and he just wanted sex." I could see the water swelling in her eyes. I leaned over and hugged her.

I whispered in her ear,

"Ann, I want you, all of you...your mind, your body and your soul. I want all of you and

I can wait until the day you are ready to be with me physically," I said.

My soliloquy was bullshit. My heart was hardened, and I didn't give a damn about her feelings. Her lips trembled as she listened to me pedal a boat load of garbage. She hung on every word. I watched her as she hung her head. She cried, and I stretched my eyes in an attempt to make tears fall.

"Thank you, Terrell, thank you...You are my gift. I believe you are the man I have been waiting for it." she said.

Love will make you change who you are and become who you are not. I fell in love with a church and a way of life. It caused me to forget who I was. I donated money out of love. I bought into the concept of giving until it hurt. I bought into the concept of sacrifice. I saw my mother overwhelmed in bills, but she loved that ministry, so she gave her all and gave all she had. She did it out of love.

Sitting there looking at Ann Marie, I knew love would make her open those virgin thighs. She said I was her gift and I knew that her heart was in it. I felt her words. If I had a heart, I would have been touched. If my conscious was working, I would have let her go...but the thought of that pristine virgin vagina got the best of me. I squeezed Ann a little tighter and kissed her forehead. We talked for hours. We stayed on her couch until the sun colored the morning sky in orange. At some point, we both fell asleep on her couch. I woke to her head resting on my bulging zipper. I was careful to control my urges. This would not be the night...and I was okay with that. Sometimes life is a sprint and sometimes it's a marathon. You have to know what race you are running. I wanted her, but I needed to be patient. I looked down at my watch. It was four in the morning and I needed to pick Yolanda up at five. She worked a ten-hour shift. I nudged Ann.

"I need to leave before it gets too late," I said.

She walked me to the door. We hugged again, and I held

her tight. Her body went limp in my arms. Her breasts rested against my body. I felt her body, it was relaxed, calm and safe. I knew soon I would taste her love.

I raced to pick up Yolanda from work and we drove back to her place. That day, I began to see Yolanda differently. She was fat instead of curvaceous, she snored instead of purred, she waddled instead of switched. I was uninterested.

"Are you coming over tonight, Terrell?" she asked.

"Nah I'm going home," I said.

She was quiet when she pulled up to my mom's house. I leaned over and kissed her on the cheek. She smirked as I closed the door. In my mind, I thought who cares. She drove home, and I went into my mother's house. My mom was waiting up for me.

"What's up, Momma?" I asked.

She told me that my cousin had come by to talk to me about joining the army. I was interested but I was overweight. The thought of joining the army intrigued me, but I knew I had a long road ahead in order to make weight. I pushed the thought out of my head as laid down for the night. My focus was on Ann Marie and cracking the code to her untouched vagina.

I met Ann Marie off and on for the next couple of weeks. I was the consummate gentleman. She enjoyed being with me and being around me. I kept the perfect distance from her. I stayed close enough to get her attention but far enough away to make her pursue me. There is a point in a relationship when the power changes. That point where the sovereign becomes the dependent. Ann Marie had crossed over. She didn't want to lose me now. She was tired of being alone and willing to lower her standards to keep her man. I could feel the change in our conversation. Our talks were less and less about "The Lord" and more and more about her untouched honey pot. We talked less and less about church and more about how far we could go without sinning or how much she could take without giving in to temptation. She constantly told me that she would resist until marriage. That was a challenge to me. We talked about kissing spots and touching spots or if fingering was considered sex. I loved the conversations. It showed that she was interested, and her body was tired of being a virgin. Our phone conversations became so erotic she told me she had dreams of me pleasuring her. I had a routine I followed. I called Ann every night at the same time. Women love consistency. My attention was unwavering. One Friday night, our conversation took a titillating turn, allowing me to know I had finally broken the lock to her well preserved pearl.

"Hello, Ann."

"Hi, Terrell." Her voice always changed whenever she heard me on the line.

"What are you doing, Ann?"

She replied, "Sitting here, thinking about you. When can you come over?"

I loved that question. "When do you want me to...come?" I asked.

Every time I asked that, she paused. I imagined she was thinking about my thick creamy release trickling down the inside of her thighs.

"You can...come whenever you want," she replied, responding to my tease.

I smiled so hard my dimples hurt. "We are talking about the same thing right?" I laughed.

Giggling, she said, "I'm sure we are."

"I have a question to ask you," I said.

"Ask me whatever you want, I'm an open book," she responded.

I hesitated. I knew what I wanted to ask, but I didn't want to seem overly interested in sex. I paused for a while.

The silence between us was broken by Ann stating,

"Ask me whatever you want. I really don't mind."

"Okay...So, um, do you consider oral sex as sex?" I asked, attempting to sound shy.

She paused to gather her thoughts. I imagined she even blushed a little, never having considered having a tongue massage her love spot.

"I don't know, Terrell." Her hesitation made me change my tactics and become more aggressive.

"Ann, I can't take it anymore. I need to release. Being around you and not touching you is killing me. I want you.

We don't have to have sex, but I need to feel some intimacy," I scoffed.

Almost whining she replied,

"Terrell, I know it's hard on you and I'm trying...please." She begged with pain in her voice. She didn't want to lose me. She didn't want to be alone again. She was willing to do anything to keep me and I could hear it in her voice.

"Ann, I come over and I sit there kissing you and holding you, but I want to..."

I stopped short of saying anything obscene. It would be better to wait for an invitation before you delve into an erotic conversation.

"You want to do what, Terrell?" She gave me my invitation.

"Ann, I had a dream last night and it felt so real that I woke up reaching for you. In my dream, we were sitting on your couch. I leaned over and kissed your neck. You laid back and let my hands explore your body. I touched your breasts and slowly dragged my tongue down to your nipples. As you slid back on the couch, your short skirt rose up your thighs. My fingers found their way in between your legs, gently pressing against the outside of your panties."

I could hear her breathing heavy over the phone as I painted a sensual picture.

"Slowly, I slid my tongue down the center of your stomach, dragging it carefully across your naval, closer and closer to your panty line..."

"Terrell, STOP!!" she screamed.

She knew where the conversation was going.

"Are you coming over or not?" she asked.

"Ann, I can't take these dreams," I said.

"Okay, Terrell, just come over and we will talk about it," she said.

"Okay, Ann, I'll come. What time do you get off?" I asked.

"Terrell, we have been talking for months and you don't know my schedule?" she asked.

I wanted to say, "Of course not." Why the fuck would I care about her schedule? She had reached the point where she was willing to lower her standards to keep her man. I was ashamed for a little while, but the thought of her spotless lady part got the best of me. I called Yolanda and asked to borrow her car. She hadn't talked to me in a few days. She was excited to hear from me.

"Sure, you can get my car. Do you want me to come pick you up now?" she asked.

"Yes, please. Thank you. I love you, Yolanda," I said.

It wasn't one of my finest moments. Those words spilled out unconsciously. I didn't realize what I said. Yolanda arrived before I was dressed. I knew I had fucked up by telling her I loved her. I changed into some jogging pants and a t-shirt. Yolanda asked if I was in a hurry.

I said, "Yes."

She asked me to drive. I sat down in the driver's seat. She

never asked where I was going. She never asked what I needed her car for at that hour in the evening. She trusted me, and I was content on violating that trust. I was undisturbed at the thought of reinforcing a false sense of confidence in her. She only had one question for me as I buckled my seatbelt.

"Did I mean it?" she asked.

"Did I mean what?" I said, pretending to forget my *I love you* fuck up.

"Do you love me?" she asked.

I thought to myself, "Oh shit." I fucked up. I had broken a rule. You never say "I love you" if you don't mean it. That word was responsible for wars. O.J. loved his wife and he was killed. She's dead because of his love/hate for her. I had to commit to the lie or risk losing my ride for the night.

"Yes, I do love you," I said effortlessly.

"Take the long way back to my house," she commanded.

She made it very clear what her intentions were. She moved my seat belt aside and pulled down my pants and briefs. My cock went instantly hard. I was so aroused at the way she went for my erection. She wanted it! She had a little jacket to cover my dick with whenever a truck was coming by on her side. She got in a comfortable position and was cupping my balls. Then, she squeezed my shaft and teased my head. I had pre-cum almost instantly. But we were in this for *the long haul* – or as long as I could last.

I told her, "I love you holding my cock."

I took my seat belt off for just a second in order to pull my pants down further. The design of this car did not make it easy for a blow job. I was content to let her fingers explore. She continued to play with my balls, but most of her focus was on masturbating my stiff shaft. I was absolutely loving it. I asked if she wanted me to start playing with her pussy.

She said, "I want you to cum."

This gave me the total green light to let it all out. She started to really twist and turn on my dick. I asked her to go up and down on it faster, and she was all too happy to oblige. She was watching my face closely as I exploded in her mouth while I pulled in her driveway. She swallowed all of it. I went into her house to clean up. I still had a long ride to Ann Marie. I came out of the bathroom and she leaned in for a kiss. I turned my head, giving her my cheek to kiss. She hadn't rinsed her mouth out or brushed her teeth. Kissing her would have been like sucking my own dick. I walked out of the door smiling.

I called Ann Marie as I pulled out of the driveway. I tried to contain my excitement as I drove down the interstate, but my erection pushed through my sweatpants.

I arrived at her house and knocked on the door.

She yelled, "Its open, Terrell."

I walked in and locked the door behind me. I expected her to greet me with open arms and wet panties, but she was in another room,

"Where are you, Ann?"

She said, "I'm upstairs."

I hesitated, waiting on an invitation to come up to her room. My heart sank when she said, "I'll be right down."

I sat on the couch and began flipping channels. I heard the floor creak as she paced back and forth. I looked up, following her nervous footsteps with my eyes. I sat patiently wondering if she had changed her mind. Finally, she walked down the stairs. She stood on the last step and motioned with her finger for me to come to her. She had on an oversized t-shirt that stopped mid-thigh. Her hair was down, falling off her shoulders to the center of her back.

I walked over to her and gave her a hug, pressing her against the wall. My erection was firm, and she felt all of me through my thin sweatpants. I could feel her body twitch as I positioned my bulge between the center of her thighs. I leaned down and kissed her lips. She kissed me back. I pulled her close to me and picked her up. She wrapped her legs around my waist as I carried her over to the couch. I sat down and laid back as she positioned herself on top of me. I reached behind her, unclasping her bra. She let me slip it off without any hesitation.

My cock was throbbing with anticipation, but I didn't want to rush. I reached down and put her left nipple between my tongue and the roof of my mouth. I fondled her right nipple, placing it between my thumb and index finger. Her body's reaction let me know that her breasts were her weak spot. She spread her legs and began to slowly grind her pelvis against my hard erection. I slid my hands down her back and over her ass cheeks. She spread her legs even more. Her panties were wet as I pulled them to the side. My finger slid inside her with ease. She had never been penetrated by anyone's fingers other than her own, never touched by hands other than hers. Her virgin honey pot dripped with her love juices. I could feel her warmth grip my finger.

I stroked her slowly with my hand. My fingers plunged in and out of her virgin puss. She kept her eyes closed as she kissed me, slowly spreading her legs wider and wider. My erection was so hard it felt like my skin would split under the pressure. I needed to release. I pulled down my sweats exposing my rock-hard manhood. She grabbed it with her hand, still unsure if she wanted to make love to me. She opened her eyes and we both paused.

I could read her face. I knew that look. It was the look of uncertainty. It was the look of fear. It was a look that said she needed reassurance. Reassurance that I would not just be her first but be her only. She had waited so long for love and only wanted love to explore her untouched parts.

She rested her head against my chest and said,

"Terrell, I can't."

My body screamed "BITCH WHAT THE FUCK" but I kept my silence.

I needed to be understanding. I needed to be caring. I ran my fingers through her hair and said,

"Okay, Ann, I understand."

My mind was racing. I wanted her now and nothing but a true commitment would get

me what I wanted. A true commitment is what I needed to give her. I sat up on the couch. My mind was racing. I needed to figure it out. I sat silently for about fifteen minutes. She was the first to speak.

"I guess you think I'm a tease?" she asked.

In my mind, I said, "Hell FUCKING yes." But my mouth said, "No, not at all...I'm not temporary Ann. I'm your forever. I can wait."

She said, "Are you sure?"

I could see her wiping the tears from her eyes. I tilted her chin upward and brushed away her tears, looked her in her eyes and told her,

"I'm not going nowhere. I love you and I'm yours."

She leaned over and hugged me as I reached down and pulled out a stick of big red gum. I noticed the shiny silver wrapper and a thought entered my mind. I stuck the gum in my mouth and began to fold the silver foil. I fashioned it into a circle as she asked me what I was doing. I slid off the couch and got down on one knee in front of her.

"Ann," I said, "the only thing that's temporary is this ring. I want you in my life and I want you to be my wife...marry me...accept this token ring as a symbol of my love."

She cried and said, "I will."

The tears continued to fall down her cheeks. She excused

herself and went upstairs to the bathroom. I thought to myself,

"Damn, I'm going to fuck the hell out of Yolanda when I get back to Orangeburg."

I heard the bathroom door close behind her as she stood at the top of the stairs, calling down to me, "Terrell, come here."

I walked over to the bottom of the stairs and looked up. To my delight, there she stood, wearing nothing but her silver foil ring. Her body was amazing. Ann took pride in her small frame and as I slowly walked up each step, I could see the benefits of her work. My eyes gazed at her perfectly manicured feet leading up to her well-toned calves and slim muscular thighs. Just below her panty line was a well shaven strip of hair hiding her protruding puss lips. Her stomach was flat and had a hint of the beginning of a six pack that led up to two very hard silver dollar nipples.

I stood two steps below her and placed my tongue on her stomach. Slowly dragging it down to her panty line, my hands reached around and grabbed her round ass cheeks. I leaned into her body and placed my tongue on that freshly shaven landing strip. She was wet, and I could taste all her juices. Her moaning only intensified my arousal. My tongue pressed against her clit as I slid my middle finger inside her. Her moaning and shaking made my erection almost painful. I wanted to jump up and viciously pound her pussy into submission, but I stayed on my knees. Sucking her, licking her, fondling her with my tongue while kneeling on the stairs. I grabbed her ass cheeks, pulling her hard against my face. She grabbed the railings to maintain balance as I continued pushing my tongue in and out of her. She had only heard about the pleasure of oral sex but never experienced it. I was her first.

She squealed and went limp as her orgasm covered my face. Her wet puss juices dripped from my chin. I licked my lips as her moans turned to whimpers. I stood up and we walked to her bedroom. She laid down and I laid on top of her. Slowly, gently, I massaged her virginity with the head of my thick, hard cock. Up and down her slit, I slide my thickness. Up and down, teasing her and tempting her. Slowly, I pushed my tip inside her. She wrapped her arms around me and pulled me close to her body.

She whispered in my ear "Don't stop."

I pushed myself further inside her. Her fingernails pressed into my skin as I slid all the way in. I did it. I had tapped the untapped. Tasted the fruits of the untouched. I was exploring the unknown and it felt good. Grinding her slowly felt so good. Her eyes were closed, and her moaning was in rhythm with my strokes. Her pussy contracted on my swollen erection as she surrendered herself to me. Her feet were flat, and her knees were bent as I laid between her legs. I felt a flood of cum squirt out of her as she orgasmed for the first time from penetration. I reached up, placing the palms of my hands in hers. We gripped each other's hands, making a tight fist as I thrust myself harder inside her.

She tilted her head back and screamed "Oh God" as my strokes became more firm, harder and harder as she screamed louder. My body tensed, and I could feel my manhood swell. I was about to release my load.

"Where do you want this cum?" I asked.

She said, "Inside me."

I exploded in her. My thick cream filled her as my body went limp. I rolled over, lying on my side next to her. She turned on her side, facing me.

"I love you, Terrell," she said.

I thought to myself, "Love? Fuck that shit, I just got the pussy."

I laughed internally. "This was the worst sex ever," I thought to myself. I'll never be anyone's first again. She didn't know shit sexually. She just laid there with her legs spread. No doggy style, she didn't ride me, no rolling over on her back or side or stomach...nothing. Who the fuck just lays on her back? This was too much fucking work. I was done with this lazy former virgin pussy. I still considered myself a gentleman and I didn't want to hurt her feelings. Even though I knew I was done with her newly unwrapped puss, I controlled my response and said what I knew she wanted to hear.

"I love you too, Ann."

I closed my eyes as she leaned in and kissed me. We made love a few more times that evening. I knew I was not coming back after this night, so I wanted to cum as often as possible. I couldn't sleep soundly because I knew that Yolanda would be wondering where I was with her car. I laid next to Ann, staring at her sleeping body, trying to think of an excuse to leave. I could have spent the night, but I didn't want to. The challenge was gone, so why bother lying to Yolanda about her car? It wasn't worth the trouble, plus I was ready to go. My craving and desire for Ann left with the explosion of my penis in her untouched fruits. I looked at her differently now that the mystery was gone. I laid there, playing back in my mind all of those conversations that we had had. She was clingy and aggravating now. The more I thought about all of those late-night talks that ended with me masturbating or rushing over to Yolanda house for a late-night booty call, frustrated me. I reached out and nudged her firmly enough to wake her.

"Ann, you got any juice?"

She yawned. "What kind of juice?"

I thought to myself, "Apple and orange juice are common. I needed something that would get me out of the house."

"Grapefruit is my favorite," I said.

Her eyes were still closed as she cleared the sleep from her voice.

"No, I don't have any juice at all."

"I'm going to run to the gas station right quick." I had no intention of coming back, ever. She opened her eyes and said,

"Baby, don't leave."

Her high pitch voice annoyed me. Ejaculation had

changed things. It was a regular pussy now, nothing special at all, and I could get regular pussy anywhere. I leaned over and kissed her forehead.

"I'll be right back, Ann."

I tried not to reach for my pants too fast. I sat on the edge of the bed, wondering how long to pause without giving away my intentions. I slipped on my sweatpants and stood as I pulled my shirt over my head. I kept my back turned to her. I could feel her watching me. My shoes and keys were downstairs. I turned and looked at her before I walked down to get them.

"I'll be right back."

It wasn't convincing at all and I could tell from her stare that she knew. Fuck it, I didn't care. I had to go. As I sat on the couch, I could hear the floor creak under her footsteps. She was up, pacing. I walked out without saying anything. I smiled as I walked to the car, thinking about my clean getaway. I cranked up and put the car in gear before checking my phone. I had sixteen missed calls. Yolanda was blowing me up all night. I pulled into a gas station near Ann's house. I was hungry and wanted a snickers bar before I got on the road. I sat behind the steering wheel and enjoyed my candy bar. I love chocolate after sex. I finished, cranked up, and pulled out in the opposite direction of Ann's house. My phone rang just as I turned onto the interstate. I picked up. It was Ann.

"Hello?"

There was a long pause before she said anything.

"Where are you honey?" Her voice was unnervingly calm. I wasn't in the mood for a long dramatic call, so I lied.

"I'm on my way back to your house."

She paused again, and then in a cryptic tone she said,

"No, you're not."

It was something about her voice that made me look in my rear-view mirror. I didn't see any cars that resembled hers, so I angrily said,

"Yes, I am. I got something to eat, but I'm coming back."

She paused again. "I know you got a snickers bar and you ain't coming back."

I felt a chill rush over me. I checked my rear-view mirror and both side mirrors before I asked, "Where are you?"

She said, "Pull over."

"Pull over?" I repeated. "Hell no, I ain't pulling over. Where are you?"

Her demeanor changed that instant. She began crying and screaming,

"Why are you doing this to me, Terrell? Please stop the car."

I remained silent on the phone and kept driving. This was the exact bullshit I was trying to avoid.

"Terrell, please stop. Where are you going?"

I maintained my silence, slowing down to see if any other car slowed, then speeding up to see which car sped up. She continued badgering me to stop.

"Please, Terrell, don't do this. Terrell, just stop the car. Terrell. What did I do, Terrell?"

Over and over, she continued to plead for me to stop. The more she talked, the faster I drove. After about ten miles, her temperament changed and her pleads turned to chilling threats.

"If I ever see you again, I'm going to kill you!"

I felt a knot in my chest. I believed her, and it frightened me. The realization of what I had just done gave me some discomfort. I hung the phone up and began to weave in and out of traffic. I was trying to put distance between me and every car on the road. I drove nervously, checking my mirrors. She continued to call my phone.

I picked it up once more only to hear her say,

"I'm going to gut you like a pig."

Something inside me wanted to pray. I was scared. I had thoughts of her pulling up alongside me and riddling my body with bullets. I got to Orangeburg and turned down a few back roads. I was in my home town now and I knew the streets. I pulled into a vacant lot and turned off my lights. I sat quietly and alone, watching every car that passed. Time ticked by slowly. I watched every set of headlights that came in my direction. As I sat there in that vacant lot, an uncontrollable nervous laugh came over me. I thought about who I feared and was hiding from. I outweigh this chick by a hundred pounds, yet here I sit, cowering in the cut on the side of the road.

I said out loud, "Man, fuck this shit," as I cranked up the car. I continued to talk to myself out loud, trying to build my confidence.

"I'm not sitting on the side of no damn road, hiding from no chick."

I drove around a little longer before deciding to call Ann. She picked up on the first ring and I asked,

"Where are you?"

"Don't worry about where I am, where are you?"

I knew that she had never been to my house, but my nerves and fear convinced me that she somehow knew where I lived. I hung up the phone without saying anything else. I drove straight to Yolanda's house and parked the car in her backyard. I didn't want any more confrontation that night, so I reclined the seat back, locked the doors, and went to sleep.

Early the next morning, I was awakened by a knock on the window. I looked up into Yolanda's angry eyes. I had already thought out my lie and knew how to play the entire situation. I gazed back at her with a frown just as ferocious as hers.

As soon as I unlocked the door, she snatched it open, screaming,

"Where the hell you been, Terrell?"

I looked up at her and said, "What the hell you mean?"

My tone and obvious anger disarmed her. I could tell she was expecting a different reaction. I knew I had her off balance, so I continued my assault.

"All night I have been knocking on your door. Who the hell you had in there?" It was a question I already knew the answer to. There was no way she would have brought another dude to her house.

She looked at me and said,

"Terrell, you know I didn't have anybody over here. I didn't hear you knocking." I listened to her playing into my hands.

"You are lying, Yolanda. You know what, I'm sick of this bullshit. Take me home."

"No, wait. Terrell, I swear I didn't have nobody here."

I knew her self-esteem was low, and she was in love. Whatever I said to her would only increase

her anxiety and fear of losing me.

"Then why didn't you answer the door?" I asked.

I could see her mind racing trying to figure out how to deescalate the situation.

"I didn't hear you knocking, Terrell."

I paused for a moment. I knew she was telling the truth. I knew that she loved me with every inch of her soul. My conscience was hard and seared. It wouldn't allow me to let up, so I pressed her.

"Take me home, Yolanda."

I wanted to hear her beg me to stay. I wanted to hear her plead for my presence. And she did.

"Don't go, Terrell. I'm sorry."

For some reason in my mind I felt justified. I had stooped

to a new low and I didn't see it. We left the parking lot and went inside. I knew she would please me. I knew she wanted to give herself to me sexually to make up for the night before. It was easy now. I understood how to manipulate, and my heart was growing colder and harder. She made love to my body. She wanted to prove herself to me and I felt it. I felt her care and concern. I felt her love, but most of all, I felt her fear. I felt her fear of being alone again, her fear of being single. Inside I laughed.

A few months passed since I last saw Ann Marie. I turned on the radio station, but she was off the air. Every now and then I would get a shiver when I saw a car that resembled hers. Eventually, she became a footnote to a story about conquests. I grew tired of Yolanda as well, but my financial situation had become worse. I was broke, didn't have a car, and was living with my mother. I needed this chick. I wanted to leave, but I had no way out. My dependency on her was too great. The Army was the answer to my prayer.

CHAPTER NINE

My cousin, Sherrod, was my best friend. He was the only person who knew all of my secrets and often encouraged me to get away and start fresh. I always blew him off. The country was at war. Why would I want to join the army? His persistence, along with my empty pockets, caused me to rethink my position.

After weighing the pros and cons of joining the Army, I went down to the local recruiter. He looked at my overweight, out of shape body and laughed. That was the first time in a long time I felt ashamed about anything. It was also the first time I focused on something other than women. I went to Sherrod, who was a Staff Sergeant in the army, and asked for his help. In my mind, all I could hear was that recruiter laughing at me. That, along with getting out from under Yolanda's thumb, was my motivation.

I pushed my enormous frame out of bed each morning. I listened to my cousin tell me how pitiful my fat ass was because I couldn't make it around the track one time. He ran me until my feet blistered. "Up the stairs, around the track, do some pushups, do some sit ups, look what you did to your body!" he spouted. Every day, I wanted to fight his ass. Every day, I thought "If he calls me fat ass one more time." I laugh now because that was my motivation. Anger had propelled me to work harder. Anger was my new best friend. It motivated me to make my naysayers liars. I was determined to make that recruiter see how much I wanted this. And I did it. I initially lost 60 pounds. I entered the army weighing 280. After basic training, I lost another 55 pounds. I came back home 110 pounds lighter than when I left, and my lust for women had gone from bad to worse.

CHAPTER TEN

At 28 years old, I started over. I joined the army. I went to basic training at Ft. Jackson. I loved still being in South Carolina because it was home. My cousin had prepared me for the basic training bullshit, so I was not shocked when I got off the bus and men in uniform with round brim hats were yelling in my face. The yelling, constant pushups, and getting up early didn't faze me at all. I was older than all the other recruits in my class and after 10 weeks of their teenage bullshit, crying, whining and bitching, I was ready to move on. Millennials make me sick.

My next training station was in San Antonio, Texas. I finally had some freedom. No more basic training constraints. My focus immediately returned to hitting the club and chasing chicks. I misrepresented myself. I didn't want to seem like the old guy, even though I was the "oldest" guy in the barracks. So, I lied about my age. I shaved a few years off to hang with the younger crowd. I told everyone I was 23 when I was actually 28. I felt old and out of place. I had been in church so long, I had no idea how to be young. The last time I heard rap music was in high school. It was 2002 and I was still stuck in the 1990's. Kids were listening to Nelly, Young Buck and Eminem. Jay-Z, The Blueprint was high on the charts along with Missy Elliot's Under Construction. I had no idea who any of these people were. So, my first time in a club, I stood with my back to the wall, waiting for the DJ to play some Tone Loc, De La Soul, or even Beastie Boys. It didn't happen. No Schoolly D, Kool G. Rap or EPMD either. No one was doing the electric boogie or hammer time; the new thing was Shake that Monkey and Soulja Boy. I was out dated, and it made me hate the church even more. I had missed a lifetime of fun for cult ministry. The more I thought about Bishop Prangles, the more I hated him. His pretentious, self-serving ministry was the reason I was stuck in a fucking time warp.

I only went to the club one time in San Antonio. I felt out of place. My Saturday nights consisted of watching movies and trying to have more than two drinks of Hennessey without passing out. Bars were more my speed. The crowd was a little older and I didn't have to worry about looking like an ass doing the Roger Rabbit or the Kid and Play Kick step. They nicknamed me "Two Drink Minimum" because after two drinks, I was semi-fucked up. I liked the older crowd.

Women were less inhibited. On some occasions, they even bought me a drink. I wasn't used to that. Being from the South, I was used to pursuing women. Now women were more liberated and they approached me. I liked it.

Periodically, Ann Marie would call me, and so would Yolanda. I ignored them both. I was brand new and women approached me now. My new physique got me a lot of attention and I worked on it every day. Even though I was physically fit, though, I was empty inside. Despite all of the turmoil and dysfunction from my marriage, I missed my children. My life was changing fast. I went from being a small-town country boy to living in a much bigger world. The end date of my training was approaching. I was going to be sent back to South Carolina for a while. Tanya had already begun the divorce process. I pretended not to care. But I did. I hated her, but I loved her at one time.

At night, I would lay in my bed, wondering about the children growing up in a broken home or growing up with their daddy gone. Thinking about someone else taking my role in their life hurt. At that moment, I resolved to try and fix things with Tanya. I wasn't interested in reconciling the marriage, only reuniting with my children. I knew I couldn't have one without the other. So, trying to make amends with Tanya made sense. My heart was conflicted. I hated Tanya, but I wanted my children. I grew up without my biological father and my step dad was cruel. I didn't want my children to experience that same kind of cruelty. I would have done anything to keep them from facing those horrors. If reconciling with their mother was the key to having them, then why not? After all, if my mom could live with an abusive man for years, then I could put up with a no-good woman for my children. I couldn't stomach talking to Tanya, so I emailed her.

August 17, 2003

Dear Tanya

I know we never really got along. I'm writing you this email because I'm afraid if I try to talk to you in person we'll start fighting. It seems we manage to agree on one thing, and that is we don't belong together. I know when this relationship changed, and I know who caused it. None of that matters when children are involved. I've decided I can't continue to allow my hatred for you to push me away from my children. I realize that our lives are too interconnected for me to just disappear and not try and make this work. I will try for the kids. If you need to get in touch with me, my phone number has not changed. I think it would be better, though, if we could stay in touch via email. I loved you once and I don't know if I can ever love you again, but I will tolerate you for the children.

Always, Terrell

August 19, 2003

Dear Terrell

What kind of email is that? You say you want to be back with me and you talk to me like that? You left me, I didn't leave you. Me and these kids are a package deal. You should be on your hands and knees begging for forgiveness. You had sex with one of my church sisters. And now you want me back. Well you are going to have to do more than write an email. You hurt me Terrell. You haven't even said you were sorry. If you can't do that then the answer is NO!

Tanya

August 21, 2003

Dear Tanya,

I hate that you are so self-centered and stuck in your own world. You aggravate the shit out of me. You know I am saying shit that makes sense. It makes me so angry that you always put yourself before the kids. It's as if they are not important to you. Well they are important to me. And I am willing to stay with you for them. I'm not selfish, maybe you should stop being so self-centered and think about the kids for once. You want me to apologize for deciding that I don't want to be cheated on or lied to or have my shit stolen. Grow the fuck up. I ain't apologizing for shit. I ain't sorry for shit. Actually, I am sorry for leaving my children. And they are who this is about. NOT YOU! Get the fuck over yourself. Let's just get back together and see where it goes.

Always Terrell

August 26, 2003

Dear Terrell

You are so nasty. You don't know how to talk to people. You need to come back to church. Your language is horrible. God is not pleased with you. You didn't just leave me, you left the church. You left everything. Just because I was on a video or in pictures with a "minister"? He's a man of GOD. We weren't doing anything. For all you know, we could have been handling church business. Us being in the bank together doesn't mean anything. You don't know if we were doing church stuff or not. And even if I did do something, it was because you weren't a good husband. You and your emails are mean and hateful. You didn't care about me. You never did. I'm not going to be with someone like you just for the children. If you want me then you need to be a man and talk to me right. Otherwise, just leave me and my children alone.

Tanya

August 28, 2003

Dear Tanya

FUCK YOU! You are selfish. I didn't realize it for a while, I thought it was me. All during our marriage I thought I wasn't paying attention to your needs. The entire time I looked for faults within myself. Then I realized the truth. The truth is that you were just too lazy or ignorant to meet me halfway. You call me mean and hateful. Nah chick, you got it all wrong. You have said the most horrid things to me, things that make others gasp in disbelief. You lied, you cheated, and you stole. Then you blame me. You tell me that your attitude is a reaction to the way I act towards you. You don't have the guts to JUST SAY you were wrong. This is because you ain't woman enough to A) have enough consideration for another human being and B) own up to your FUCKED UP behavior. You have no respect for me. I set up some boundaries with you. I told you that I will be your husband for the sake of the kids. What the fuck is wrong with that. Ain't like you got shit else going on. Get your fucking life together before I take the deal off the fucking table. You ain't the fucking prize...I AM

Always Terrell

September 03, 2003

Dear Terrell

My life is together. I don't need you, I need your child support. You sound so full of yourself. You think you are a prize...you're NOT! I don't have to apologize to you. I asked God to forgive me. And you don't know if I did anything, you just think I did. At least I'm still in the church. At least I still go to church. You don't even go any more. You ran off and joined the army and didn't even have the guts to tell me. I had to find out from Yolanda. Yes, I talked to Yolanda and she told me about ya'll. How do you think I felt going to your HOE to find out where my HUSBAND was? You are not a good man or a good person. I knew you were gonna come back. I knew it.

Tanya

September 05, 2003

Dear Tanya

FUCK YOU! *I don't even know how to start this letter. I began writing to you because every time we talk, I feel anger. I don't want you back, but I will tolerate you back in my life to be with my children. You have not changed. You are still the exact same way you were. I won't go into how trifling you are or how much of a piss poor mother you are. These are things you already know, and I have no business reminding you of them. For the most part life with you wasn't all bad. The sun still shines even when it rains all week. I want you back with the same conditions. I think that as grown-ups we should be able to agree on stipulations that will benefit our children. Being without you doesn't hurt me at all, knowing that I won't see my children every day does. I was fine before you came into my life and I will be fine long after you are gone. I will never be alright without my kids. So, let me be honest. I don't want to be your husband, I want to be your partner. I want to be your teammate. I'm telling you this because honesty is the best policy. Oh, and I don't give a damn what you and Yolanda talk about. Go have lunch together and reconcile...why the fuck would I care?*

Always Terrell

September 09, 2003

Dear Terrell

Why are you talking to me like that? The army has changed you. I've got news for you: that is not how a man talks when he wants a woman back. You are clueless. You are a coldhearted sinner. You are coldblooded, cruel and hard-hearted. The bible says, "Ephesians 4:31 Let all bitterness, and wrath, and anger, and clamor, and evil speaking, be put away from you, with all malice." You are nasty and bitter and mean. All those things define you. I messed up, but you are taking it too far. I don't like who you are becoming. You sound like your daddy.

Tanya

September 10, 2003

Dear Tanya

BITCH YOU DON'T KNOW MY DADDY! I should have known better than to think honesty was going to be valued. Now I realized that me being completely honest with you screws everything up. I should have lied to you, I should have played like I did all the other clueless bitches. I should have treated you like what you are...a side piece. But I didn't. I approached you with honesty. But you don't understand that concept. You can't fathom honesty because you don't know how to be HONEST! It's okay...I know who and what you are and I'm okay with it. For my kids, I will be OKAY with it. For my kids, I will be OKAY with you. I was NEVER in love with you, I loved you. The church was small, and all of the other girls were taken. You were the only one there that was single. I see that now...you don't. I can admit that. I can also admit that I wasn't perfect. And even though your imperfections FAR exceeded mine, I am still willing to forgive and overlook yours. I'm not asking you to be back in my bed. I'm asking to cohabitate for the sake of the kids. Who I used to be is not who I am. I'm not the fat guy with low self-esteem. I'm not blindly led by your preacher. I am not in love with you...but I do have a love for you as the mother of my children. That's as good as it gets. I'm sorry if that's not enough for you. It is enough for our children. So, for once in your life think about someone other than yourself.

RYAN T. MOORER

Always Terrell

September 12, 2003

Dear Terrell,

I don't know if I should do this or not. A part of me is saying yes but another part of me is saying you need to change. You are different now and I don't know if I can be with you like you are. You sound so mad. You are unforgiving. None of those emails say I'm sorry. So maybe if you start the next email with I'm sorry then we can look at trying to get together. Maybe we can talk with the Pastor and find a way to start over. But you need to apologize.

Tanya

September 13, 2003

Dear Tanya,
FUCK YOU!!

Always Terrell

I WANTED MY CHILDREN BACK AND IF IT MEANT overlooking her faults, I was willing to do it. Nothing else mattered to me. But apologizing to her was where I drew the line. I'd rather drown than apologize to her. I no longer loved her, but I could fake it for the kids. I rationalized it in my mind. I could fake love, I could fake care, I could even fake a relationship, but what I couldn't fake was an apology. Not to her. There were limits to my hypocrisy and apologizing to her was pushing the boundaries of those limits.

The last day of training came. I packed, ready to move back home to South Carolina. My Drill Sergeant came through the barracks handing each soldier their orders. He handed me mine and I glanced at it, eyes wide in excitement. OH, LORD, I'M GOING TO HAWAII! All I could think about was the women, the beaches, AND THE WOMEN! Fuck reconciling with that thieving ass bitch! Let the bitch divorce me. I don't give a fuck! I threw every letter in the trash. I wasn't going back to that bullshit woman and our bullshit marriage. Besides, you don't have to be married to your children's mother to be a good father. FUCK YOU Tanya...ALOHA BITCH!

CHAPTER ELEVEN

As soon as I got off the plane, my eyes widened. They call this place paradise and I ain't never leaving. I was greeted at the airport by Hula Girls. I was in full uniform when a scantily clad Polynesian woman placed stringed flowers around my neck.

"Aloha, welcome to Hawaii."

"Thank you, I'm Specialist Terrell. What is this you put around my neck?"

"Specialist Terrell, I am Hualani, and I have placed a lay around your neck."

I immediately became a 7th grader again. The mention of the word "lay" made a juvenile smile cross over my face. I snapped back to adulthood, but my mind was still in the gutter.

"Hualani, that is a very pretty name. What does it mean?"

"It means, Heavenly Fruit."

The dog inside me wanted to say,

"I bet your fruit does taste Heavenly."

But I didn't. I had just got off the plane and I would have plenty of time to whore around the island later.

I was assigned to the Army hospital. My Sargent met me at the airport. He knew what I was thinking and warned me to be careful. He gave me all the precautionary stories about soldiers who fell into problems on the island. I heard him, but I wasn't listening. After all, this was HAWAII.

My first day in training I met Kisi. She was (at the time) the prettiest girl I had ever been with. She was fresh out of college, young, spirited, and inexperienced in life. Her hair was long and straight. She liked to wear it down with the ends curled. She had on blue jeans that hugged her hips. And boy did she have hips! Hips so curvaceous that I dedicated the beginning of a poem to her...

"She's got thick lips and thighs,
light brown eyes,
the kind of hips that will make a grown man smile,
and when I first saw her,
my impression was My, My, My,
I hope that I can lay between those thick thighs for a while."

She was a nurse, so she could wear civilian clothes. She

had on a North Carolina A&T sweatshirt. That was my opening. Her rival college, South Carolina State University, was in my hometown. I approached her during our break, striking up a conversation about how my school was so much better than hers. She laughed. I looked into her hazel eyes and felt my body tremble. Her ample breasts pushed through her sweatshirt. Her body was thick, but her waist was small. She loved wearing jeans because they showed off her frame. She was about 5'5" and she wore CK1 perfume. I didn't ask her out right away. I needed to scope out the hospital before I committed to one girl. We exchanged numbers and spent the next couple of days texting each other.

A few weeks passed, and I finally got up the nerve to ask Kisi out. We wanted to explore the island. We spent the evening getting lost in Hawaii...laughing and talking. She told me everything and I listened attentively. She had only slept with one man in her entire life. She had never experienced oral sex before. The last guy never went to church. He cussed like a heathen. I watched her face as she talked. I saw her disappointment and hurt. I watched as her life so freely rolled off her lips. My mind was spinning the entire time. She needed to feel love but she also wanted respect. She wanted someone open and honest. She wanted a boyfriend...and dammit, it was going to be me. We settled for dinner at the Cheesecake Factory, and after dinner we went for a walk on the beach. It was her fairytale and my scheme. We playfully walked in and out of the water. The tide lapped at our toes as we held our shoes. We paused for a moment...it was a scene from a chick flick I had seen once. I leaned in and kissed her on the lips.

"Thank you, Kisi, for a wonderful evening."

She blushed. "Thank you."

I leaned in for another kiss. It was a soft kiss as I barely pressed my lips against hers. Her hazel eyes in the moonlight looked amazing. We walked back to her car holding hands. It was late as we drove back to post. She suggested that her apartment was closer, and I could sleep on her couch. I paused before I answered. I wanted to at least give the appearance of being a gentleman.

"Are you sure? I don't want to disrespect you."

She laughed. "Oh I am sure, and you will be on the couch."

I laughed inwardly, knowing that I would be on the couch only half the night. We entered her high rise and took the elevator up. I held her hand silently. We went into her apartment and I was impressed. Everything was high-end. Kisi had excellent taste. Plush couches and goose down comforters. My mind sunk to a new low. Kisi worked nights and I needed a place to take the new chicks I had met on the island. This place was picture perfect. I needed to be her boyfriend and do boyfriend things so I could have access to the apartment.

That night we sat up for a while watching TV. We shared a few laughs and a kiss or two. I laid down on her couch and watched as she walked into her room. I watched her ample ass shake from side to side, calling me, teasing me, inviting me. I listened as the shower turned on. I imagined beads of hot water touching her skin. I imagined the steam rising and fogging up the bathroom. I imagined drops of water trickling down her body, across her breasts, and down past her navel. I wanted my tongue to trace every trail that the water traced. I wanted to suck the water of her nipples. I laid there on that couch, a victim of my own imagination. My erection grew harder and harder wanting to feel her. Soon, I heard the water stop. She walked to the door wrapped in a white cotton towel.

"Do you need to shower?" she asked.

My erection pressed against my pants so hard that it hurt.

"Yes, I do need a shower."

I walked into the bathroom. I could smell her scent. The smell of cocoa butter enticed me even more. I got undressed and stepped into the shower. It was cold. I made sure of it. I stayed there until my erection went soft. I stepped out of the shower, not realizing that I didn't have any other clothes. I wrapped myself in a towel and walked out to a glorious surprise. There she was, lying on her bed, holding a small egg-shaped vibrator between her thighs.

Trying to appear unfazed, I calmly said,

"I'm going back to the couch."

With her eyes closed, she said, "That's fine."

I watched as her body enjoyed the vibration against her

clit. Her body shook with the anticipation of her climax. I watched as she trembled. Her moaning and groaning caused an instant erection. I grew harder and harder as her moans became louder. She exploded on the bed. Watching her satisfy herself made me want her. She wanted me to want her. The temptation was too much. I walked over to her bed and knelt down on the floor. I grabbed her legs and pulled her towards the edge of the bed. Spreading her legs wide, I could smell her juices mixed with the fragrance of pomegranate soap. Freshly washed and shaved. My tongue salivated at the thought of replacing her silver bullet. I didn't go back to the couch that night. I stayed there on the side of her bed, massaging her clit with my tongue. Her body rewarded my efforts. My face was glazed with her juices. She tasted so good. She pulled me on top of her. I made love to her body that night. Slowly grinding myself inside her, touching her hair, and planting small kisses all over her neck. The passion was intense. She hadn't been touched in a long time. She felt my love. She felt all of me inside her. She fell in love that night. I laid next to her, watching her watch me. I smiled because I knew she felt special.

The next morning, my mind raced at the thought of being in Kisi's apartment. I was introduced to a new social network site called Black Planet. I uploaded some photos and got a few hits. Kisi's apartment was the perfect place. It was a high rise that overlooked the ocean. From the balcony, you could see a beautiful Hawaiian sunset over the ocean. The evening skies burst with orange and red as the sun retired each evening. The soft glow of the sunset over the clear blue ocean was picture perfect each night.

The next few months were a blur. I spent my time learning Kisi's work schedule. She worked twelve hour shifts from seven to seven. I made all my dates at nine to give me time to hide all of her visible personable things in the closet. I continued to play the role of the good boyfriend, dropping her off at work, bringing her lunch and making sure she had breakfast in the morning. That was my job. I kept her off balance. There was a buffet of lonely women in Hawaii and all of them wanted a military man. All of them wanted to be loved. It was laughable.

I met Lallana on Black Planet. She was native to the island. I sent her a picture of me coming out of the pool. I was in shape and the water dripped off my body, making me look like I was straight off a photo shoot. She was a beautiful Polynesian woman, a native of the island. She wore her long black hair in one braid that fell down the center of her back. She was slim with breasts that seemed to be too big for her body. Her eyes were slanted, giving her an Asian appearance, but her skin was tan and dark. She was gorgeous. I wondered why someone so sexy was on a dating website. She could have had any man she wanted.

Our very first date was a romantic evening at Kisi's house. I drove Kisi to work that night and surprised her later on the job with a bouquet of flowers. I was careful to hide the other roses in the trunk...they were for Lallana. Kisi was so excited. She was never the type to show public affection but this night she couldn't contain herself. I accepted her hug and kiss in front of her gushing coworkers. I knew they were jealous. Treating a woman well in front of her female friends is like fishing. You are just casting bait for the next fish. I left Kisi's job to pick up Lallana.

Lallana walked to the car dressed in all black. She was beautiful. She worked out regularly and her body screamed for attention. Her black satin dress hugged her petite frame, accentuating her ample breasts. Her thick, swollen nipples pushed through her dress. The moonlight seemed to dance off each one. To my delight, she wasn't wearing a bra. I tried to smile inwardly only, but I couldn't contain my excitement.

She sat down in the car and asked,

"Why are you smiling?"

"Lallana," I said, "you are amazing."

She blushed. Her perfume smelled fresh. It was the scent of just stepping out of the shower. My body reacted to her fragrance. My erection was firm as I anticipated laying between her thighs. We drove back to Kisi's apartment. I stood behind Lallana on the elevator with my hand around her waist. Her back pressed against my chest and her firm ass pressed against my erection. She smiled when she felt the size of my pleasure pressed against her. The elevator stopped, and we entered the apartment. She was impressed.

"Is this your place?" she asked.

"Yes, it is," I proudly responded.

"You live here by yourself?" she asked as she looked around.

"Yes, but I could always use a roommate."

She laughed and walked out onto the balcony, looking out over the ocean. She whispered softly,

"I could get used to this."

I stood behind her, turned her around, and looked into her eyes. I told her,

"I would love to have you here with me...I need a woman like you to fill this empty space. The space in my heart and in my home."

Staring into her eyes, I leaned in and kissed her lips. She kissed me back. I pulled her close to me, pressing my chest against her chest and her pelvis against my erection. I wanted to lift her dress and push myself deep inside her, but I exercised control. The night was young, and she was too attractive to just fuck and leave. I needed to impress her. We stood on the balcony for a while and then I walked her back into the living room.

"Are you hungry?" I asked.

"Yes."

"Good because I'm going to cook for you."

"You can cook?" she asked in astonishment.

"Yes, I can. I'm good in the kitchen and great in other areas of the house."

Sarcastically, she said, "Yeah, your bathroom is real clean. Do you do floors and windows, too?"

"You got a quick tongue and a smart mouth, and I like that."

"My tongue can do so many other things."

I was almost speechless. This beautiful woman was coming on to me. She was hitting on me. I walked over to take the ground beef out of the refrigerator. I looked back at her and said,

"I think I want to experience the way you use your tongue."

She laughed. "Maybe you will."

In my mind, I gave myself a pat on the back, acknowledging my own successful cockiness. The thought of her full lips wrapped around my thick cock, swallowing it inch by inch, made me as excited as a child on Christmas morning.

"I'm making spaghetti and salad. Are you okay with that?" I yelled from behind the counter.

"Yes, I love spaghetti. No man has ever cooked for me before."

Bragging, I looked at her and said, "I ain't no regular dude."

I watched her watching me. I put on a great show. I boiled the noodles, browned ground beef, and opened some sauce. Really there is nothing else to do when making spaghetti. I poured her a glass of wine while she watched me cut the lettuce and tomato for the salad. Soon, dinner was ready. We sat down at the table and I served her. Amazed at my culinary skills, she continuously complimented me on the meal. We flirted throughout dinner, laughed and made small talk here and there. After dinner, we walked over to the couch. She sat close to me as I flipped through the channels, trying to find something interesting to watch. She grabbed the remote and turned the TV off. I watched as she walked over to the radio and turned to a slow jams station.

"You want to dance?" she asked.

I laughed. "I don't dance, sweetheart."

"Don't dance or can't dance?"

I smiled and said, "Both."

She pulled me up off the couch and held me close to her. My body moved with the rhythm of hers. I leaned down and kissed her. She kissed me back. My hands touched her, rubbed her, exploring every inch of her body. She walked me backwards over to the couch. I was prepared for a sensual moment of love making. Teddy Pendergrass played in the background, telling us to *"Turn off the lights."* I leaned back onto the couch, expecting her to slowly take off her clothes and lay on top of me. My eyes glazed over as she pulled her vibrator out of her purse. I was floored at how fast she lost all her inhibitions. It seemed out of character for her. I laid there on the couch, frozen, while she slowly sashayed toward me, swinging her hips while her eyes focused on the growing bulge in my pants. She straddled me, pulling up her dress...

then leaned over and whispered in my ear, "I'll do whatever you want. I want to please you."

Not allowing me to speak, she slid her hands down to my waist and began unbuckling my pants. I grew harder and harder as she wrapped her hands around my exposed dick. She looked me in the eyes and said, "Lie back, shut up, and enjoy the show."

Something about her giving me orders turned me on even more. I lied there as she got down on her knees and buried her face into my hairy groin. I felt the back of her throat contract as she took all of my tools into her mouth as far as it could go without gagging. She started sucking hard on it, tickling my swollen head with her tongue. My throbbing bulge began to swell into a solid rod as I laid back, moaning in delight. I enjoyed being teased and having my inner thighs wet from her saliva. Her blow job was sloppy, and I could feel my balls getting wetter and wetter. She stretched her jaws as wide as they could go. I gripped her head, driving my erection into her hungry mouth. She didn't want me to cum. Just as she felt me swell and my body tense, she sprang to her feet and walked into the kitchen. I watched her as she leaned over the kitchen table, spreading her legs and gripping the edges of the table. She was taunting me, teasing me, calling me...asking for it. I walked over behind her and placed my hand on the small of her back. I pushed myself deep inside of her tightly hidden treasure, filling her sweet, juicy walls. With each deep stroke, I pounded her tight puss hard, slamming my balls into her backside. I could feel her body instantly began to thank me for the attention I was giving it. I watched as she reached down with one hand and I heard the silent buzz of her vibrator. I was turned on even more.

"Oh God, you feel *soooo* good," I said, half moaning.

"Shut up and fuck me!" she screamed.

I kept driving myself hard inside her. It had been a long time since her body was moved to react like it did. It craved attention...it craved pleasure. Her wetness began to trickle down her thighs and I felt her knees buckle. She pushed me away and walked over to the couch. She motioned for me to sit back down on the couch. She slid down on my hard rod, straddling me and looking into my eyes while her tongue slid into my mouth. She began moving up and down on top of me, entering, locking her hands around my neck, resting her forearms on my broad shoulders. I held her tiny hips, pressing her hard against my dick.

"I'm going to cum," I moaned.

"Don't cum yet," she said.

"I'm bout to cum," I moaned.

She slapped my face hard as she stroked my dick. "Don't cum yet," she screamed. I gripped her waist hard and exploded. She rode me harder, the sensation was too much for me. It was a tense sensation that I had never felt. My toes curled so hard that my feet cramped. I begged her to stop, but she didn't. She dug her nails into my back as she exploded on my dick.

"Damn," I said. "What the fuck was that?"

She laughed and rolled over onto the couch. A few minutes later, I heard her breathing change. She was asleep.

My alarm rang at 4 am. I nudged Lallana, telling her to get up. I needed to have her out and erase all traces of her before Kisi got off work. She woke up to my lie about having to go to early morning PT. I cut short her suggestion to stay in the apartment until I got off work. I pretended to have a deadline, giving myself an excuse to rush her out of the apartment. We rode the elevator down in silence. I ushered her to the car and hastily drove her home. My adrenaline surged as I rushed back to Kisi's house to clean up before she got off. I made it through traffic and got back to the apartment. I spent the next hour cleaning and wiping down the entire house, meticulously putting everything in the exact same order it was in before she went to work. The alarm rang again. It was 6:30, time to go get Kisi.

I pulled up in front of the hospital. Kisi walked out, gushing with pride. I leaned over and kissed her.

"How was work?" I asked.

She smiled. "You got all these women jealous. They've been hating all night over my roses."

I smiled and put the car in gear. "Do you want McDonalds, or do you want me to cook you breakfast?"

She said, "You can cook for me and I'm going to do something for you."

I was tired of sex and I wasn't in the mood, but I had to

put on a show. We drove back to her apartment. We walked in, she undressed and got in the shower. I went into the kitchen and made pancakes. She came out of the shower wrapped in a towel. She stood near the counter watching me flip pancakes. I smiled within. Girls love watching a man cook. I fixed her a stack and poured some juice. My mind was racing, trying to figure out how to get out of sex. I just wanted to sleep. I gave in. We went into the bedroom and laid down and I went through the motions. Bad sex is better than no sex. I rolled onto my stomach and went to sleep.

I woke early and logged onto Black Planet from Kisi's laptop. I was looking for Lallana. I sent her an instant message to let her know that I enjoyed her the night before. She emailed me back almost immediately.

"I'm not your bitch or your girlfriend. We fucked get over it, and have a nice life!" I stood there puzzled, trying to figure out what just happened. Talking to myself, I confirmed that the sex was good. Dinner was great, and I was romantic and passionate. I began questioning myself. Did she just treat me like a chick? Am I chick? Did I just become the victim of a "one and done?"

I emailed her back. "Damn that was cold as hell."

She responded, "Thank you for the funky time." I couldn't contain my laugh.

"Is that Darling Tanya?" This chick just dumped me with a Prince lyric. Fuck it. I logged off and rolled back into bed with Kisi.

Two weeks after Lallana, I met Tua. A week after Tua, I met Lili-okalani. They all visited Kisi's apartment. They all tasted my spaghetti and they all tasted me. I had perfected a system of rotation and I was proud of it. A rotation of one-night stands. A carousel of women. My heart had grown cold. I tried hard to forget the principles and values I had been taught. Church was a distant memory and Deacon Terrell was a name I hadn't heard in a long time. Years had passed, and the feeling and inspiration of church was a footnote. Living in the moment made it easy to forget the past, but every so often when I was alone Mamma's words seemed to find me. Sometimes I would hear her saying, *"The LORD your God goes with you; he will never leave you nor forsake you."* The thought of the Lord being with me used to make me shiver in fear. I felt like my relationship with God had ended. That life was a fading memory.

Kisi woke early one Sunday morning. We had been sleeping together for months. And for months, I rotated a steady stream of women in and out of her apartment. Most of our Sundays were spent having a late breakfast and doing relationship things: walking on the beach, watching movies or spending a lazy day in bed. This morning was different. I woke to her nudging me and suggesting that we go to church. It had been a long time since I set foot inside a sanctuary. I felt something inside compelling me to go, so I agreed. I threw on a pair of jeans and a button up shirt. We drove to church in silence. The only understanding I had of church was from

Trueway. The only Preacher I knew was Bishop Prangles. I hated church. I hated the feeling of judgmental eyes looking at me. I hated feeling like everyone knew what I was doing, like my soul was completely exposed. I had walked away from the things of God for a reason, and now my hypocrisy was sinking to a new low.

We walked into the Kingdom Life Temple of Deliverance late. The preacher was already up speaking. It seemed like he stopped as soon as we entered the building. Kingdom Life was a mega church. It was furnished with four 75-inch flat screens on each wall, a balcony, and what seemed like thousands of people. Maybe I was paranoid to think that the sermon paused because of me. The songs were inspirational, and the sermon caused tears to well up in my eyes. I hadn't felt that way in a long time. I choked back tears. I didn't want to feel anything.

Hearing that minister say,

"God is still with you, regardless of your circumstances," made me angry. He looked in my direction as I fought back the tears and said,

"Never forget God loves us all. Man will let you down and the entire world may turn on you, but God will never let you down. He loves you."

I felt myself become angry. I felt anger at my situation. Where was God when my back was against the wall? Where was he when my ex-wife was stealing my money? Where was he when she was fucking the church minister? Where was he when Momma was being kicked and punched and stomped? Where was God when Prangles was misleading the church? Where was God when Prangles was using my money to enrich himself while our car was broken down and our lights were turned off. As far as I was concerned, God had turned his back on me which didn't motivate me to lift my arms in praise to him. Maybe I'm wrong for thinking this way, but "I'll be wrong" was my attitude. Bitterness, resentment and frustration had led me to that point. It was an anger that I had never dealt with. I felt abandoned by God. No matter how I tried to direct those frustrating feelings toward the pastor of my old church, I still questioned why God allowed it. I wasn't ready to face these feelings within myself, so I walked out.

Kisi ran behind me as I stormed off towards the car, calling out,

"Terrell, wait what's wrong with you?"

I hesitated. I knew what she wanted. She wanted me to break down and discuss past experiences. I was not ready for that hallmark moment. I didn't want to give her a Lifetime movie experience. So, I kept quiet.

She looked at me. "I'm not leaving church, Terrell."

I wanted to say, "Fuck it, I'm leaving." But I was in her car.

"Okay, Kisi, we will talk when we get back to your place."

I walked back in and sat quietly. I thought I could tune out the entire service. I was familiar with the routine. Choir singing, asking for money, preachers screaming, asking for money, church shouting, asking for money. My cynicism kept my mind closed to any thoughts of a reunion with Deacon Terrell. I had buried that guy and engraved his headstone with "The blind worshiper." I smirked as I likened the arrangement of services to the same monotonous rituals that I had seen in so many other congregations. The same methods that were the catalyst for turning me against the entire institution of organized religion. The sermon was about faith. I listened to the preacher bellow:

"What's the name of your faith? What do you say when you're down? Is it I really want to Lord, but I can't right now? Is it I wish that I could, or I hope that I can? But I gotta play these cards, cause God you dealt me this hand. See the name of your faith is what you believe when your back is against the wall and you wiping tears with your sleeve."

As he spoke, I tried hard to ignore the tugging in my heart. I didn't want to feel anything. But the poetic melody of his words found their way inside, chipping away at my hardened heart. I wanted my bitterness to overwhelm me and to push me to that angry place where I cared about nothing. It didn't happen. The mind has many rooms. Locked away inside of one of those uninhabited spaces was misplaced thoughts and experiences of a life unlike the one I was presently living. Deep down, past the anger and feelings of disdain, past the contempt and the resentment, past the hurt and distrust, lived someone waiting for a chance to reemerge.

Unconsciously, tears flowed down my cheeks. I hadn't

become aware of these buried feelings until that moment in church. That's when I realized that my strong hatred for Prangles was great, but it wasn't greater than the connection I had with God. I missed that connection. I missed the feeling I felt when the joy of praise took over my body. I missed the congregation responding to the spirit. I didn't want to reminisce, but I couldn't control my thoughts. My mind flooded with the past life of Deacon Terrell. A life that I thought I had buried within the dark, unexploited caverns of my psyche. I squirmed in my seat as a familiar feeling urged me to respond to the ministry in a way that felt like ancient history. I resisted. Deacon Terrell was dead to me. That life and lifestyle was dead to me. I could feel Kisi's eyes. She was watching me. She was watching my internal struggle as it played across my face. She placed her hand on top of my hand to comfort my hidden pain. I looked down at my watch, screaming internally, "When is the damn benediction!" Then we stood.

"May the Lord watch between me and thee, while we are absent one from another, AMEN?" And it was over. I looked at Kisi and smiled as I walked out. She stayed behind to do the traditional meet and greet. I wanted no part of it. I leaned my back against her car waiting on her to unlock the doors.

I thought to myself,

"Damn, I need my own ride."

I watched Kisi walk across the parking lot. Something had changed. I didn't like her anymore. I managed to attach my feelings of discomfort to her. It was her fault I was in that church in the first place. She unlocked the car and we rode in silence to Tony Romo's. We walked in silently, grabbed a table and waited for the waitress.

Kisi broke the silence,

"You're not talking to me?"

I looked at the menu in silence. The waitress came over. She was a slender white girl with long brown hair. She was annoyingly perky with a high-pitched voice. All the waitresses wore black slacks and white button up shirts. Kelly, our waitress, was flat chest and flat assed. So much so that her pants looked as though they sagged in the buttocks area. Her pleasant temperament was an over compensation for her homely look.

"Hi, my name is Kelly. Welcome to Tony Romo's. May I take your order?" she asked with a smile. It was a well-rehearsed greeting.

"Hi, Kelly. I'll have sweet tea, and I know what I want already."

Kisi looked at me with confusion on her face. Those were the first words I had uttered since we left the church. She motioned to Kelly and said,

"I'll have sweet tea also, and I'm ready to make my order as well."

"Okay, ma'am, you go right ahead," Kelly said, taking out her pen and pad.

"Give me the number nine, baby back ribs with the beans and macaroni."

"I will have the same," I said.

Kelly reached down and grabbed our menus, saying, "Okay, two number nines. I will take your menus and be right back with your drinks."

Tony Romo's was fast and cheap. Kelly's promptness with our order broke the twenty minutes of awkward silence at the table.

"Here you go, two number nones with sweet tea. Do you need anything else, hot sauce or ketchup?" she asked.

I always get offended when a white person asks me if I want hot sauce. It gives me an uneasy feeling. It's the suggestion that all black people eat hot sauce. Not looking up, I said,

"No thank you, Kelly. We are good."

As she walked away, I turned my full attention to my plate.

"I'm starving. I shouldn't have skipped breakfast." Kisi stayed quiet.

"I was hungry when we left the house, but my stomach is talking to me now," I continued. Still she said nothing.

"These ribs are good as hell." Nothing.

I used both hands, forgetting any resemblance of etiquette. Kisi looked at me with disgust.

"Aren't you going to wipe your hands?" she quipped.

"I'm eating ribs. I'll wipe when I'm done," I said sarcastically.

The place was crowded for a Sunday. She continued in her judgmental tone,

"You are eating like a country Bammer."

I laughed,

"You love this Bammer, and you definitely love this hammer."

I took a sip of my tea through a straw. She put her fork down, wiped her mouth and said,

"Everything is about sex with you. Why did you walk out of the church like that?"

I was had been waiting for this question. I reached down to pick up my napkin. I wiped my mouth and put the napkin back across my lap.

"Kisi, as much as I pride myself on being able to articulate an explanation for any action that I do, I am at a loss for words."

"What do you mean by that?" She seemed irritated. "See, this is why I hate the military. It teaches you guys to bottle up shit and then you explode later. What's going on? Why did you walk out?"

I didn't want to talk about it, but I did.

"Kisi, I used to be someone else. I was Deacon Terrell. I was someone that lived church, believed church, ate, slept and bled church. I opened the doors and I closed them."

I went into a lengthy explanation of my old church life.

She looked at me as if I was telling her a plot from a movie. Her eyes fixed on every word that fell from my lips. When I finished my tale of woe, we sat in an uncomfortable silence. She didn't know what to say and I wasn't sure if I had said too much. And then she started.

"Terrell, I realize that you're not who you used to be and I'm not suggesting you return to that life. In many ways, I admire the fact that you were strong enough to leave that tough situation, but you have to know that God didn't do it. You've had a horrific experience from day one. While I wasn't there to witness what you've been through, being mistreated or humiliated, I understand your hurt." Quietly, I listened.

"You see, Terrell, I had to learn to fend for myself. My parents weren't there for me." When the conversation shifted to her, I started feeling some kind of way. My frustration deafened my ears to everything she uttered. Who the fuck did this pompous bitch think she was? How was she going to ask me about myself and then give me her fucking sad story? I didn't want to hear this shit.

My mind raced as I thought to myself, "This self-absorbed, pompous ass, fake ass chick is not gonna lecture me." I remained silent for the duration of our meal. Kisi continued to talk. She had an air of confidence in her words. She fooled herself into believing that she was getting through to me. Kisi wanted a husband. She was thirsty for someone to plant a seed in her voluptuous, childbearing hips. She wanted an upstanding, church going man. She wanted Deacon Terrell, but he was gone. Long gone.

We finished our meal and walked to the car. I had an uneasy feeling driving back to her place. I struggled with ending the relationship. My heavy heart wasn't for losing Kisi, but for losing that apartment that had become synonymous with my routine. It was a part of me and I loved it. The way that so many women reacted to the view overlooking the Pearl Harbor memorial was magical. Her pillow top mattress along with the goose feather pillows made so many women swoon. How could I leave such luxury to move back into the barracks? The ride in the elevator to her apartment was long. We walked in. Kisi poured two glasses of wine and we took our usual position, cuddling on the couch, just as we had done every Sunday night for the past several months. Kisi's body relaxed, and I could feel her weight shift, leaning more against my body. I heard her breathing get heavy and watched as her head began bobbing. I frowned. The little things bother you when the relationship is over. I flipped through the television channels. *Sex and the City* was on. She loved this movie and I fucking hated it. A bunch of white, uptight women talking about screwing. What the fuck? Kisi woke up. She had seen this movie a hundred times before and she wanted me to watch it with her, AGAIN. She grabbed the remote when I turned the channel and nudged me.

"Hey, you," she said. "Wasn't that Sara Jessica Parker?"

"Uh huh," I murmured.

"Why did you turn it? I love that movie."

I raised my head, stretched, yawned, and rubbed the back of my neck, saying,

"My bad, Kisi."

She laid her head back on my shoulder just as Carrie began to hit Mr. Big with flowers in the middle of the streets of New York. Something clicked inside of me as I saw Mr. Big attempting to explain himself.

"You know something, Kisi?" I was angry. I'm not exactly sure why my mood had changed so fast, but I was pissed. My frustration had built up in my head, causing my outward reaction to reflect it.

"What? What's wrong with you, Terrell?"

"Kisi, I think I'm falling out of love with you."

"What?" She sat up quickly. Her voice reflected her surprise.

"What's wrong with you, Terrell? You've been so distant since church."

"Distant," I scoffed. "Nah, I'm not too distant. I'm tired."

"Tired of what, Terrell? I do everything for you."

My anger grew. "What the fuck do you do for me? I don't owe you shit."

I sat up on the chair and reached for my glass of Moscato on the side-table, took a long swig, and set it back down. I rubbed my chin between my thumb and finger, unsure if I really wanted to go down this road. Kisi always found that habit, along with my silence, annoying.

"What are you thinking?" Kisi asked.

"Are you serious?" I said. "You think I owe you."

"I never said that, Terrell."

In my mind I was searching. I needed to start an argument and storm out, but the hurt in her voice made it difficult to be an asshole to her.

"What are you thinking?" Kisi asked again.

"I'm falling out of love with you, Kisi." I was firm.

"What have I done to upset you, Terrell?"

She stood and moved to the chair next to the couch. She placed both hands on her knees and looked directly at me. Still rubbing my chin, I remained silent. My lips parted in an attempt to give a long, well thought out speech about the struggles and trials of young love, but only a sigh fell from them. She shook her head and looked at me.

"WHAT IS IT!" she screamed.

"Nothing," I said. "I was going to say—"

"Say what?" she interrupted. "What?" she screamed. "What were you going to say, Terrell, spit it out."

"Well, you know, a separation could work out for the best," I stammered

I tried to focus on the movie as I spoke. I knew that looking into her teary eyes would weaken me. *I heard Samantha Jones say, I'm gonna say the one thing you aren't supposed to say. I love you...but I love me more. I've been in a relationship with myself for 49 years and that's the one I need to work on.* God, I fucking hate this movie.

I continued my thoughts.

"Separation could work, Kisi. Not seeing each other anymore so seriously is not a bad thing."

"But why, Terrell?"

"Kisi, the thrill is gone."

I hated breaking up. The crying, the sobbing, the begging, the explaining...the talking and talking and talking. I wished I had a fast forward button. Kisi laid her head against the back of the chair.

"Is that really how you feel, Terrell?"

"Yes, Kisi."

"But you just fucked me this morning, Terrell. I just paid for dinner at Tony Romo's. I introduced you to my church members, Terrell. You think I'm stupid? I know you're fucking other bitches...Terrell."

Her mood grew darker every time she said my name. It was like she was building herself up and saying my name made her stronger.

I thought to myself, "Here we go." The typical accusations of it must be another female.

"Kisi," I interrupted. "I didn't mean we wouldn't see each other. We can still fuck, I just don't want to be in a relationship. But we can still see each other every now and then."

Kisi shut her eyes and stopped talking. She grabbed her

temples and slowly began to massage them. It wasn't uncommon for her to get a headache, and after the conversation we had, I could tell one was developing. Her emotions were all jumbled up. Her forehead had wrinkled into an unnerving frown.

"You want another glass of wine?" she asked.

"Sure," I said.

I began to think to myself, "This went better than I thought it was going to." I dreaded the break up. I hated the long drawn out conversations and the battle to remember every lie I had ever told. Women are so much better at recalling every fucked-up thing a guy has done. Kisi got up and went into the kitchen. The cast iron skillet she used to fry chicken in the night before was still on the stove. It was her mother's pan. I heard a loud clang as she threw it in the sink to quickly wash off the left-over oil. I looked back at her as she winced again from the pain in her head.

"My head is spinning," she said as she lifted the pan by the handle from the dishwater. I picked up the remote just as *Carrie Bradshaw said, "Sweetie, you shit your pants this year. I think you're done."*

I said out loud,

"No *Sex and the City* today. I'm done," and changed the channel.

Without a sound, Kisi walked over to the sofa, raised the skillet as high as she could, and brought it down on the back of my head. I clenched my teeth as I heard her scream,

"I LOVE THAT MOVIE!"

I slumped sideways on the couch, unable to move but still coherent. She picked up the remote, changing the channel back to *Sex and the City,* and walked back into the kitchen. I could feel saliva trickle from the corner of my mouth as I lay motionless. Kisi turned on the water in the sink and began furiously scrubbing the pan. Because I am an avid *CSI* and *Law and Order* fan, I assumed she was washing off any DNA fibers. After rinsing and drying the pan, she put it away and walked back into the living room. I didn't move, and Kisi didn't know if I was breathing or not. Thirty or forty minutes had passed, but it still felt like my brain was rattling inside of my head. Kisi sat in the chair beside the couch and cupped her head in her hands.

"What have I done, what have I done?" she moaned.

She began to cry. Her shoulders shook with each sob. After some time, she straightened up and wiped her eyes with the back of her hands. I was conscious of my surroundings but afraid to move. Kisi heaved a sigh and shuddered.

"Fuck it, I hope you die," she said aloud to herself. She bit her lip and said, "I'll tell you something else too nigga, you better stop slobbering and bleeding on my fucking couch. And I ain't never gonna fuck with you again."

Slowly, I rolled over onto the floor. I lied face down on her rug. She got up and turned out the lights. She left me there, lying on her floor with a golf ball size knot on my head, blood streaming down the side of my face. Slowly, I began to feel the life refurbish in my limbs. I managed to get onto my knees.

"I'm going to kill this bitch," I thought.

I could barely stand. I placed both hands on the couch, pushing myself up, managing to stagger to my feet. The room was spinning as I placed one foot in front of the other. I thought about running into that room and choking Kisi, but I knew in my condition she would whip my ass. I made my way to the apartment door and walked out, closing it behind me. While pushing the button and waiting on the elevator, I heard Kisi lock the deadbolt. I shuddered. I thought she was coming to finish me off. The elevator chimed, I walked in, pushed the button and sat on the floor. I watched the doors slide closed.

I awoke the next morning in my barracks bed with a heavy headache. Dried blood caused my face to stick to my pillow. My head throbbed, and the lights hurt my eyes. I was sure I had experienced a concussion and needed hospitalization, but my pride prohibited me from going. I was an ER medic and going to the hospital meant explaining what happened to my superiors. So, I suffered through the pain. I got up and started to walk towards the washroom, maintaining my balance by holding onto the bed post, then the wall, then the door, and finally the bathroom sink. I stood there looking in the mirror, examining the large lump on my head. I sat down on the toilet, trying to recollect what had happened last night and how the hell I had gotten back to my room. Everything was a blur. The last thing I remembered was getting off the elevator and calling a cab. I'm not exactly sure how much I paid or tipped the driver. Looking in my empty wallet helped me realize that I was a generous tipper when confused. I laughed out loud, thinking of how I almost died the night before. This was the second woman that had either threatened my life or tried to take it. I laughed again. It was a nervous laugh. Looking in the mirror, I shook my head.

"Who are you? Mr. Devotional Leader, Mr. Pastor's Right Hand. Who are you?" I smiled at the idea of belittling myself.

"No one knows the demons that are in a man's heart." Kirk Franklin said that.

It's almost laughable that I remembered that quote. Somewhere in the smallest, darkest, tiniest part of my mind, church was still relevant. Even in all of my bullshit. I knew I had gone too far but I didn't allow myself to acknowledge it.

I didn't want to see it, so I said out loud, "Who am I?"

"I'm the motherfucking monster you made, you weak motherfucker. Now quit crying."

I laughed out loud again while cleaning the dried blood from my face.

"Oh well, I won't ever see that pussy again," I thought.

My casual smirk left when I touched the knot on my head. I managed to make my way out of the bathroom and back to my bed. I reached over on my nightstand and found some aspirin, left over from a previous hangover no doubt. I popped two pills into my mouth and laid my head back. I closed my eyes until my mind drifted away.

I awoke to the sound of buzzing. It was my phone vibrating on the nightstand. I reached over and picked it up. It was Momma. She hardly ever calls. I paused, trying to figure out why she was calling.

Finally, I answered, "Hey Mamma."

"Hey, Terrell."

"Is everything okay, Mamma?"

"I have some bad news. Harry died."

I hadn't thought about my step dad in years. I didn't have any good memories of him. Just about all my childhood memories of him revolved around his drinking or the beatings. I remembered countless car rides where I was scared to death, wondering if I'd make it home alive because my step dad was driving drunk. I remembered never being able to have friends over to my house as a kid because of the potential embarrassment and humiliation I would feel if my dad came home drunk then passed out in the living room (like he usually did). I remembered the time my friends dropped me off at home late one night after a football game and we found my step dad sitting in his car in the driveway. The driver's door was open, the car was running, and my dad had one leg out of the car. But he was passed out. I remembered telling my friends that my dad must have been tired from a long day at work. Children of alcoholics are quick thinkers!

In my mind, my father robbed me of my childhood and

even some of my early adulthood. We never really had a relationship. And over the years, what relationship we did have became more and more strained. For a long time, I hated my step father. Hate is a strong word, but that is truly how I felt. I resented growing up with him. I resented the merciless beatings Momma took at his hands. I hated him for not being like the other dads, the ones that would come to the football games and yell from the sidelines. He tried to reach out to me a few times, but I wouldn't talk to him or see him. Momma interrupted my silence.

"Terrell, are you okay?"

"Yes, ma'am," I said.

"Terrell, I know you are a big Army man, but its okay to grieve Harry."

I felt a twinge of anger. "Grieve?" I said in a rough tone.

"Yes, Terrell, grieve."

"Ma, after all this man has done do you, think I will shed a tear?"

She said, "Terrell, you have to let it go."

"Ma," I said, "you are blind because of this man. This is the same man that tried to throw

me down the stairs. This is the same man that beat you and when I intervened, he punched

me in the face. I was a kid and he hit me like I was a grown man."

Talking about the past made my voice quiver. I didn't want to cry. Momma's silence let me know that she was hurting also. I felt selfish. Regardless as to what I had experienced, her pain was worse. I had no right to remind her of my pain.

"I'm sorry, Mamma," I said in a softer tone.

She said, "Terrell, I should have left him a long time ago. Before he did all that to you."

"It's not your fault Ma, I don't blame you for anything."

She said, "Terrell. you have to forgive Harry for you. You have to let it go. I know that's hard to do, but you have to."

I said, "Yes ma'am."

"Terrell, maybe you can talk to someone. Maybe the Army can help you."

"I don't know Ma, I'll ask someone."

"Promise me, Terrell."

"I promise, Ma."

"I love you, Terrell."

I smiled. Momma saying *I love you* always made me smile. "I love you too, Ma."

"Bye, Terrell."

"Bye, Ma."

She hung up and I rolled over and went back to sleep.

CHAPTER TWELVE

The next morning, I called Army One Source. I requested a civilian counselor. I went off post to meet my counselor. I didn't want the Army to know I was seeing a shrink. I met Dr. Thomas in what looked like a revamped shopping center. He was a psychotherapist not a psychiatrist and honestly, I didn't know the difference. The church had always taught me to pray and ask God for help. My pastor never talked about getting help or needing help from anyone other than God. So, I prayed about everything, and the things that I couldn't pray away wasn't because I needed help. It was because my faith wasn't strong. That church made me lie to myself and so many others lie to themselves. I needed help. Going to see a therapist made me feel weak. I felt like Deacon Terrell standing in front of that old church being rebuked again. My shame caused me to pause at the door. I stood outside for what seemed like hours, holding the door handle tightly. I could see the receptionist beckoning me to come in. I took a deep breath and went inside.

There was a large woman sitting behind a glass window. In front of her was a clipboard with a pen attached to a chain. The receptionist, Nancy per her name tag, was wearing this big flowing, flowery muumuu dress that I took to be a maternity dress. She greeted me with a huge smile.

"Welcome to Fresh Start Mental Health clinic. How can I help you?"

"I need to see someone. My dad just died."

She responded with, "I'm sorry for your loss, are you *suicidal?*"

"Hell no, lady," I responded, clearly frustrated. "I'm in the US Army. I ain't weak minded

like that. Plus, I never liked him. The only reason I'm here is because I told Momma I would

come."

I saw her hand slowly slide underneath her desk. That's when I realized my voice had elevated. She was contemplating pushing the alarm.

"Are you okay, sir?" she asked with hesitation and fear.

"Yes ma'am, I apologize," I said, smiling and flashing my dimples.

I can't imagine the thoughts going through her head. One minute, I'm raging with anger. The next, I'm calmly talking to her with a smile. I'm sure she thought I was a prime candidate for mental health services. She handed me the clipboard and asked me to have a seat and fill out the insurance information. I smiled and attempted to make small talk, hoping to change her image of me.

Walking over to the paisley colored chairs I said,

"Well, I guess you won't be here much longer."

"Why not?" she asked.

"I'm sorry, I assumed once the baby was born you would take your maternity leave."

In a very injured tone, she said, "I'm not pregnant, and you do know what assuming does."

Sheepishly, I said, "Yes, it makes an ass out of me and you."

She quickly quipped back, "Not me...JUST YOU!"

She closed the glass partition.

Over the next few minutes, I filled out the paperwork and waited on the therapist. I walked up to the counter and handed her the clipboard.

"I apologize, ma'am, I didn't mean to offend you."

She smiled and said,

"It's okay, being crazy is much like being pregnant. You can't hide it for

long." She closed the glass partition and walked away. That's when Dr. Thomas walked in.

Dr. Thomas was an incredibly tall, thin man. I stereotyped him immediately as an Ivy League basketball player who was more focused on his academics rather than his game. I was somewhat intimidated. He towered over me. The huge height gap made me uncomfortable. He stood rigidly, with perfect posture which made him look even taller. He had on khaki pants that seemed to barely reach his ankles. I could see his white socks coming out of his black Rockport shoes. He wore a long sleeve white shirt with the cuffs rolled up. I thought to myself his shirt sleeves were probably too short, and he rolled them up to feel comfortable. His clothes were form fitting. I imagine it would be difficult to find suitable attire in his size.

In a low, monotone voice, he said, "Good afternoon, I'm Dr. Thomas. Everybody calls me Dr. T."

I responded, "Good afternoon, I'm Terrell." His hand engulfed mine as we shook hands.

"Right this way," he said, gesturing for me to follow him down the hall. As we walked down the hall, I saw Nancy talking to another nurse. I tried to look straight, pretending not to notice her direct stare. It was obvious...I was the new "crazy asshole patient."

We entered Dr. Thomas' office and I took a quick glance around the room. I was looking for the long couch to lay down on and the chair next to it for him to sit on like in all the movies. His office wasn't set up that way. He had a desk and two chairs. Dr. T. had several degrees on his wall. Emory School of Psychology, Duke School of Clinical Counseling, and master's in psychology from Kennesaw State. I was impressed.

"Have a seat," he said as the door closed behind us. I walked over to the same paisley cloth chairs that were in the lobby. I was a little disappointed that he didn't have a couch.

I thought he would sit behind his desk, but he sat down in the chair that was uncomfortably close to mine and asked,

"What brings you here to my office today, Terrell?"

I inched my chair over a little, putting more space between us. I'm not homophobic, but I

don't ever want my knees to touch another man's knee.

"Dr. T, my dad died, and I don't know how to feel about it."

It didn't seem to bother him that I had slid my chair over. His expression didn't change.

"Do you mind if I record this session?"

"No, not at all."

"So, tell me about yourself. Tell me about your relationship with your dad."

I skipped the personal bio and went directly to how shitty my dad was.

"I never liked how Dad treated Momma. He treated her like she was a child, like his own personal slave and punching bag as opposed to a wife. He never showed her any respect. He ordered Momma around and was not sensitive to her needs. He controlled how often she went out, called her several times a day, and would yell and scold her. He showed more respect to everyone other than my mom. And when he thought she was building up her courage to leave or stand up for herself, he beat her down, destroying any glimmer of self-esteem she had."

"Was he always abusive?" Dr. T asked.

"No, not in the beginning," I responded. "In the beginning, he thought her strong attitude was cute, but as the relationship got older, he became more and more intolerant of it."

"When did you notice his change?" asked Dr. T.

"When Mamma began to have a mind of her own, he grew increasingly irritated with her. The tension in the house got worse and worse when he lost his job. Momma would leave the house every day to my dad insulting her. He used to call her bitch or crazy, a whore, slut or stupid, and many other insults in front us. Often, we were forced to listen to him yell at her for hours, accusing her of everything. He did this to get a reaction from her. And when she didn't react, the verbal abuse became physical," I continued.

"The most confusing thing was any time he treated her like that, a few days later he would be the nicest person on earth, and that would be the time he would buy her gifts or attempt to bandage her bruises. The bruises he gave her. That behavior confused me so much. He would say sorry but not mean it because he did the same thing over and over again. He would gather us around and pray, asking God to help him. Just another fake religious fraud."

I talked for what seemed like hours. I didn't notice the tears flowing down my cheeks. I was emotionally and mentally exhausted at the end of our session.

Dr. T sat quiet during the entire session. He just let me talk. Our sessions were 90 minutes and at an hour and a half, a light blinked.

"We are going to end this session right now. How often would you like to come?"

"I'm not sure. Am I once a month crazy, once a week crazy, or twice a week crazy?" I asked with a laugh. My attempt at humor went unnoticed. Dr. T kept the same monotone, stoic expression.

"Let's do it once a week and then we will increase the sessions as needed." He reached over and grabbed his planner off his desk. Flipping through, he stopped on an open date for the following Wednesday.

"How does Wednesday at four sound?" he asked.

"Wednesday is fine," I said.

"Okay, stop by the front desk and let Nancy book you an appointment."

I stood up and said *"Thank you"* as he handed me some tissue and a small card with a date written on it. I walked out feeling refreshed. I hadn't talked about my past in years. As I approached the front desk, Nancy opened the glass partition. I handed her the card without saying anything. She looked at it and began typing. She printed out a slip.

"See you next week."

I answered back, "I'll be here."

The day had gotten away from me. I made my way back to the Barracks. The session with Dr. T was emotionally exhausting. I took a shower and then laid down. It was early evening, the sun was still up. I laid there thinking about everything. I picked up my phone and called my mother.

"Hey, Ma."

"Hey, Terrell," she said with excitement in her voice. I could call Mamma ten times a day and she would be just as excited every time.

"Ma, I went to see that therapist today."

"You did?"

"Yes ma'am, I told you I was gonna go."

"Thank you, Terrell. Thank you so much. I know it was hard for you to do that, but it will help you

out in the long run. How was it?"

"Ma, it was draining. I talked a lot about Dad."

"Do you want to talk about it?"

"Not right now, Ma."

"Okay, whenever you are ready. What are you doing?"

"I'm lying down right now, Ma. I'm really tired."

"Well did you eat something, Terrell?"

No matter what we were going through, Mamma always wanted to make sure we ate something.

"Yes ma'am."

"Okay, I love you, Terrell. Try and get some rest."

"Yes ma'am. I love you too, Ma."

She hung up the phone. I laid there staring at the ceiling, waiting to sleep. My mind drifted as I thought about the session. I felt tears roll across my ear lobes as I lie on my back looking up. I began to talk to God out loud.

"God, I used to be your humble servant. Now I don't know what to call myself. I haven't talked to you in a long time. I'm here now in need of hope. I was angry with you God. You let Momma get beat, you let her go blind, you let so many bad things happen. There are times when I felt helpless, there are times when I felt weak. I pray for hope and strength. I need hope for a better future. I need hope for a better life. I need hope for love and kindness. Some say that the sky is at its darkest just before the light. I pray that this is true, for all seems dark. I need your light, Lord, in every way. Help me. Amen."

I closed my eyes and went to sleep.

CHAPTER THIRTEEN

The rest of the week blew by. I was looking forward to Friday. I needed to get out and release some stress. The counselor, work, soldiers...they had all taken a toll on me. Every weekend, my good friend Kareem and a group of fellow soldiers went to Big City Club downtown. I wasn't a real big club person. The only dancing I ever did was shouting in the church and the occasional two step with the choir. We nicknamed Big City "Big Ratchet" because the females let loose in the club. Show your thong contests, shake your ass contests, make your titties pop contests, and shots contests were just a few of the low-level entertainment I craved after a stressful week. My battle could sense that I was having a bad week. He came to my barracks room to help get me out of my funk. I was laying on my bunk when he knocked on my door.

"What up, bruh?"

"Man, I know yo ass ain't in the bed this early." Kareem had a strong Kentucky accent.

Kareem was my closest friend out of the click we hung out with. He was a fun, no drama dude. Kareem reminded me of my brothers. His personality was laid back and non-confrontational. Kareem worked out just enough to pass his physical fitness test. He wasn't really big on being in the gym, but he had quick hands. You didn't want to try him.

"Man get up. We're going to chase these hoes." That was his famous saying every weekend.

"You must have read my mind. I need to get these streets tonight."

"That's what's up. I'm the DD tonight so you can get fucked up."

"Ohhhhhhhh HELL YEAH!" I said. "Man, you ain't said nothing but a word. Gimme twenty

minutes."

He walked over to the little bar I had set up in my room. It was really a nightstand with liquor on it. He yelled,

"Hey bruh, imma start early with one of these bottles. You already know how we do."

"That Crown is in the kitchen under the counter and I got cranberry juice in the

refrigerator." I heard Kareem laugh out loud.

"You already know."

I yelled back, "I thought you were the DD?"

He laughed and said, "I always drive better when I have had one or two in me."

By the time I came out the room, Kareem was on his third glass. I saw my new bottle of Crown half empty, so I asked,

"You still have the DD right?"

"Hell yeah, man. I'm good. A drink or two helps my nerves, plus I'm not drinking at the

club. You gonna pour you up some troubles before we leave?"

None of what he said made sense, but I wasn't in the mood to rationalize or to use good

judgement. I wanted to be reckless and careless.

"Hell yeah, imma pour me up one," I said. "Where are we going tonight?"

"Let's hit Big Ratchet."

"Shit, I'm down. Let's go get 'em."

We finished our drinks and then headed out. Hawaii was beautiful, even at night. The temperature was always perfect. As we drove downtown, we could hear the music from the club at the end of the block. The line outside Big City stretched nearly half a block. Women were in line wearing next to nothing, hoping to get someone's attention so that they could get in without paying. The dudes were fronting as much as the ladies. Each dude was trying to out floss the others and look like they had more money than they actually did. Kareem liked to crowd watch. Some of our biggest laughs came from looking at the locals all dressed up, ready to blow their paychecks. It was a circus of attention seekers with fly clothes and hot cars who lived with their mamas. HILARIOUS!

I was rocking an all-black Sean Jean sweat suit with brand new Air Force Ones. I fit right into the circus of fly attention seekers. Kareem kept it simple. Levi jeans, Ralph Lauren Polo, and sneakers. His only extravagance was his weekly fresh lineup. He was obsessed with making sure his tape up was tight. Kareem knew the bouncer, so we didn't have to wait in line. We made our way to the front of the line like superstars. The base from the music thumped through the closed doors. The sound system blared each time the door opened. We walked in.

The club was ALIVE! We paused for a minute to give our eyes time to adjust to the flickering lights. The dance floor was crowded with women shaking their asses, just like we liked it. It was the typical setting, ballers at the bar, thugs on the back wall, lovers coupled up and chicks trying to get noticed on the dance floor. We made our way to the bar, bought our standard Crown and cranberry, then turned around to scope out chicks. Neither of us were dancers but we did enjoy two stepping while some females with big asses bumped and grinded on us for a seven dollar pineapple Cîroc. We stood at the bar for a while, then Kareem noticed a fine brown skin female. She noticed him noticing her and walked over to introduce herself. When he offered to buy her a drink, I knew that was my que to leave.

I slowly made my way to the quieter side of the club, although still loud by normal standards but quiet enough to carry out normal conversations. I scanned the seats and the couches after nodding at a few wall flowers. I found a spot at a table in the corner. I sat alone, slowly sipping my brown liquor as I surveyed the girls. For some reason, they didn't seem to appeal to me that much. Just as I was continuing my gaze, I spotted a strikingly beautiful blonde, probably in her early thirties. She was dressed to kill with a very short, leopard print skirt and a black top that did little to hide the curves beneath them. She had long blonde hair that fell just over her shoulders which gave her hot body the cutest appearance. I found myself staring at this beautiful woman and after several seconds, I noticed that she was definitely turning the most heads in the club. The heated desire I had for her crept up on me fast. I watched her as she shot down guy after guy who built up the nerve to approach her while she slowly, sexually and teasingly danced alone to the on-going track. She didn't have on a wedding ring. And she didn't come to the club alone. She was joined by a guy and three other ladies who sat at her table.

The guy was out of place. He was a cornball. I thought to myself, "No way her fine ass is with that chump." This clown had on a tight Carolina Panthers t-shirt and blue jean shorts. He had on sneakers that looked like he had just finished running and white tube socks pulled up his calves. I watched him casually try to inch closer to her as she seemed to be in a world of her own. Her eyes partially closed, her arms moving so seductively. Next to her, the guy looked like a bumbling idiot. But then again, next to her, many guys would look like idiots or undeserving. Many guys, but not me of course.

As the song switched to another, the guy seemed to get bolder. His liquid courage kicked in as he tried to drag the lady out of her comfort zone and onto the dance floor. She followed suit, reluctantly and clearly annoyed. I couldn't take my eyes off her legs and sexy curves as they flowed with the rhythm of the DJ. I was so caught up in her subtle body language that I hadn't noticed Kareem standing beside me. I was startled when I heard him say, "Who are you focused on?" Seeing who I was looking at he said, "Are you serious? You are going after her? She is with a guy and we're from the South. We don't do snow bunnies," Kareem uttered.

I laughed. I had heard my Mamma say many times, "Don't bring her home if she can't use my comb." But none of that mattered at this moment.

"Bruh, there is just something about her."

Kareem laughed. "Well then get yo punk ass off the side line and in the game. Stop looking like a bitch and approach her. Scared dick doesn't get no pussy."

Somehow, his vulgar logic made sense. I made my way a little closer to the awkwardly dancing couple. I was in hearing distance and caught part of the conversation:

"...let's get trashed, sexy. I'll show you a really good time honey," the guy said to her.

"From what I can feel, it doesn't seem like you can give me, or any other woman, a good time honey," she replied sarcastically.

I almost spit my drink out at her quick tongue. There is something sexy about a feisty attitude on a woman. Listening to her give it to this clown stimulated me. I listened intently, waiting on this sheepish looking fellow to realize she was out of his league. He didn't. He wasn't that type. He was the persistent type, the aggressive type, and his response to her quick wit showed who he really was.

"What the fuck, bitch! Who the fuck do you think you are?" the guy replied angrily. He made a move to take hold of her arm, but I was lightning fast on my feet, catching his arm before it reached hers.

"Who the fuck are you, asshole?" he said, trying to get his hand released from my iron grip.

"I think you should leave dude and stop fucking with this lady. She is clearly not interested in you," I replied.

"Fuck off, asshole, this is my business," he said, finally getting his hand loose from my grip and making a fist, getting ready to fight.

"Dude, listen, I know you did your Tae Bo this morning. You can either leave on your own or get dragged out and fucked up outside." Kareem walked over and stood behind me. The DJ and the bouncers were alerted to the tension in the air. He looked around at the people, realizing he was outmatched and making a scene, and started his retreat.

"Whatever, asshole. Don't think you are going to have any luck. She is just a fucking tease," he said angrily.

Kareem waited until he disappeared before he went back to the chick he bought the drink for. I turned my attention to the lady as she was surrounded by her girlfriends. She looked at me with interest, checking me out from head to toe. I was confident about my looks. My fit body, bald head, chocolate skin and dimples always made me a winner. Plus, I was sporting a little five o'clock shadow, giving my face more character.

I approached her while she was surrounded by her friends asking,

"Are you okay?"

"Yeah, I'm totally fine. Thanks for the help by the way. He was starting to be a total creep."

"No problem. Just helping out a beautiful lady," I said, smiling at her and flashing my dimples. "I'm Terrell by the way." I extended my hand her way. "Mind if I sit with you?"

"Please do. I'm Jen. It's nice to meet you, Terrell."

Her smile radiated through me, piercing me deep, almost making me lose focus and babble like an idiot. The effect she had was indeed dangerous.

I took the seat next to her and we engaged in some small talk. She was smart, sexy, beautiful, charming and had a quality about her that deeply attracted me to her. After a while I asked,

"So, what's your poison?" I had noticed she wasn't drinking anything and wanted to rectify the matter.

She leaned in close to me and said, "Guess."

I laughed. "I'm a soldier. I'm not good at guessing."

"So am I, and I'm really good at guessing. So, let's play a game."

Unsure where this conversation was going, I hesitantly agreed. "Okay?"

"Why don't you order something for me and you'll get a prize if I like the drink," she said biting her lower lip.

"What would the prize be?" I asked, immensely interested.

"Mmmmm..." she said, scrunching up her eyebrows and thinking. She looked devastatingly cute. Each of her actions seemed to send an electric current through my body.

"Well, if you buy me something I like, you get to dance with me," she said, smiling.

"Is that a good enough prize?"

"I think it definitely is," I said, tilting my face towards her, looking deeply into her eyes. I decided to try my luck and walked over to the bar.

"Aye bruh, can I get a Crown and Cranberry and a Sex on the Beach?" I called out.

After a brief period, the bartender served her the dark orange colored cocktail, garnished with an orange slice and cherry. She eyed it curiously and took a sip from the glass. Her eyes sparkled as the mixture of flavors hit her.

"So, do I get my prize?" I asked, smiling.

"I didn't say I liked it, did I?"

"So, you don't like it then?" I asked, slowly taking hold of the glass and pulling it towards myself.

"Hey, that's mine!" she exclaimed, trying to grab hold of the cocktail.

I lifted the glass to my lips and took a sip, tasting it, much to the surprise of Jen who squinted at me, pretending to be angry.

"I think he forgot the secret ingredient."

Jen looked at me curiously. "What, did he forget about your Rohypnol?"

I couldn't contain my laughter. "That's some funny shit."

I grabbed her hand and touched the rim of the glass with her finger tip, then took another sip,

"Mmmm, now it's sweet enough." I handed the glass back to her.

She gave me little smile, leaned in close to me, her lips almost touching my ear lobe, and whispered, "That was some corny shit."

We both laughed out loud at the same time. I leaned back in my seat.

"You gonna dance with me or what?"

Smiling, she said, "Can I finish my drink first, Ike Turner?"

We both quickly finished our drinks and headed to the dance floor. I'm not a dancer but I can do the two step. I learned that from singing in the church choir. For the first few songs, we danced normally. Then, we started getting more intimate and handsy. Jen started showing her seductive moves. I tried to keep pace with her on the dance floor. I only had two moves, a fast two step or a slow two step.

The dance floor itself was quite dark, with rays of light bouncing off and again. As she started coming closer and grinding herself against me, I found myself getting hard. This beautiful damsel was doing crazy things to me.

I placed my hands around her shoulders, drawing her close to me. She came close without any resistance. We stared deeply into each other's eyes and closed in for a kiss right in the middle of the dance floor. The kiss caught both of us by surprise. Neither of us liked PDA.

My hands slowly made their way down to the small of her back, slowly feeling her curves. I inched them down and pressed over her ass, slowly rubbing and squeezing as she continued grinding against me in rhythm. I could feel the heat that generated between her legs on my firm erection.

We stayed on the floor until the lights came on. She asked for my phone and called her cell phone from it. Kareem came over and tapped me on the shoulder.

"Man, I don't know about you, but I need me some Waffle House."

He was fucked up, so I knew I had to drive. I didn't care. I had a hell of a night. I looked over and Jen's circle of girlfriends beaconed for her to leave with them. I leaned down and gave her a hug.

"Thank you for the dance."

"I hope it's not the last one she said.

"It's the first of many," I told her.

"There you go again with that corny shit. Is that a Southern thing or is that just a you thing?" she asked.

I laughed. This chick was bold, and I loved it.

"It's just me. Are you gonna call me?" I asked.

"I will," I said as I watched her walk off.

Kareem said, "Damn, bruh, you boo'd up in the club now? Where they do that at? We ain't marrying these hoes. We just give em this pipe. I ain't mad at you though, cause ol girl is a ten."

A smirk came across my face,

"You damn right she is. Now come on and lets go to Waffle House with yo drunk ass...and how the fuck you more fucked up then me, you the damn DD tonight?"

He laughed, "Shit, you already know. I got started early"

CHAPTER FOURTEEN

I woke up at 7:30 on Sunday morning, two days after that long night of dancing with Jen. It was a typical crystal blue sky Hawaiian day. The sun was shining bright as I laced up my New Balance running sneakers.

The funny thing is that the forecast for each part of the island is different. Many locals say if you do not like the weather, wait an hour and it will change. That's about right. Once I went up on a plane ride on an island tour with a friend who had just earned his pilot's license. I paid $50 for gas and we hit the skies in a single engine propeller plane from Dillingham Airfield on the north side of Oahu. We had been up for about twenty minutes when massive rain clouds started rolling in. We wanted to land but the air traffic controllers said to land in Honolulu where it was still sunny. We flew down there to find it totally rained out. They redirected us to the north again and we landed in a horrible rainstorm with forty mile per hour wind gusts.

I learned right then that Hawaii weather changes in the blink of an eye and I was gonna take advantage of this run today.

Walking out the door I heard my phone buzz.

"Who the hell is calling me this early on a Sunday morning?" I grumbled.

"This better not be work, cause I ain't working another damn weekend," I said out loud as I snatch the phone from my night stand looking at the caller ID.

It was my oldest brother. He only calls for one reason, and at that point, I wished that it was my job.

"Hello?"

"Hey. What's up, Boobie?"

I shook my head on the other end of the phone. I'm a grown ass man. Why can't I escape this nickname?

"Nothing much big bruh, what's good with you?" I asked in a low tone, knowing he was about to ask for money.

"Nothing, man, I'm just living life. I got this situation that's got my back up against the wall," he stammered, trying to build up to his request for cash. "And, uh, you know I need a small loan to try and get me over this hump. You know I'm good for it."

My blood boiled. "No you are not. You don't ever pay nobody back."

"Yes, I do, man."

"No, I ain't givin you no money."

He ended our conversation with a "Fuck you, punk ass Army boy." I laughed as he hung up the phone.

I leaned down to finish tying my shoes when my phone vibrated again. I answered without looking at the ID.

"Look, nigga, don't get yo motherfucking ass whipped. I ain't in the mood for yo bullshit. Call my fucking phone one mo time and I will fly to South Carolina and try my best to slap half yo damn face off."

I felt a chill over my body when I heard Jen's soft voice say,

"Hello?"

"Oh shit," I screamed silently, holding the phone to my side. I looked at the caller ID again and screamed,

"Shit, shit, shit, shit, SHIT, SHIT. SHIT, SHIT, SHIT, SHIT."

I heard Jen say again,

"Hello?"

"Hey, Jen, what's up?"

"Are you okay?" she asked.

"Yeah, I'm good. My brother pissed me off and I thought you were him."

"You talk to your brother like that?" she asked.

"Yeah, I do. What's he gonna do, stop being my brother?" I asked sarcastically.

"So, do you talk to everyone that way?" she asked hesitantly.

I paused before I answered. Everyone knew I was an asshole. I hear it daily. Not one day went by without a soldier or civilian worker loudly whispering ASSHOLE. Just low enough for me to hear "hole" but not loud enough for me to make out the word "ass."

So, I lied to Jen. "No, I don't talk to people that way. My brother asked me for money and then got mad when I said no. People always think that because you are in uniform you have a lot of money," I quickly said, trying to recover.

Her cautious tone changed as she agreed, "I can relate."

"What are you up to?" I asked, attempting to change the subject.

"Nothing much. I'm just sitting around the house restless, wide awake and full of energy."

"And you're going to need every ounce of that energy if you come over there," I thought to myself.

"Why don't we get together?" I asked.

"Well, I need to get someone to watch my kids. What would you want to do?" she responded.

"You have children?" I asked.

"Yes," she stated defensively, then asked "Is that a problem?"

"No, not at all," I quickly responded. "I have three children myself."

"So, what do you want to do?" she asked.

"You," I responded. "I want to do you."

Amazingly, she found my boldness refreshing. She hated

beating around the bush and the game of trying to figure shit out. We both knew what was going on and neither of us tried to pretend. We talked a little more, and she suggested that we should get a room at Pearl Harbor Navy Base since she was already up there. I told her I would text her when I got the room.

I got to the Naval base around 1400 and texted her.

Me: I'm at the room.

Her: You came up here fast.

Me: That's the only time I will cum fast

Her: Ha, Ha, what room are you in?

Me: I'm in suite 412

Her: A suite huh, did you have to take out a loan they are crazy expensive

Me: I want this to be a memorable occasion

Her: I'll be there in 45 mins

I thought to myself that was perfect. It gave me time to shower my man parts. I also wanted to set the mood with some fragrance candles. After my shower, I barely had time to light the candle before she knocked on the door. She was early. I open the door to see her long, frosty blonde hair flowing over her shoulders. She looked amazing.

I stood there staring at her blocking the doorway when she asked,

"Are you gonna let me in?"

I quickly stepped aside and nervously said,

"Come in."

Her voice vibrated with the energy of expectation as she entered, saying,

"I've been thinking a lot about you."

"So have I."

She sighed and said,

"You know, I have been feeling really good about our last date. I can't remember the last time I smiled this much. I almost wish..."

She stopped mid-sentence. I looked into her eyes with anticipation of her next words. She let the silence lingers until I said,

"You almost wish what?"

She leaned in and kissed my ear lobe, whispering softly,

"I'll tell you later."

I grabbed her by both hands and told her,

"Whatever you are feeling, I am feeling the same."

"Stop lying," she said. "I came here to fuck you, you don't have to run game."

Her response was new to me. No one had called me out on my bullshit before. I found myself intrigued by her no-nonsense, blunt attitude. There was something attractive about it. It had been a long time since I heard sincerity in my own voice. I mustered up all of the genuineness

I had in me.

"I'm serious, Jen. The instant I saw you my mind went blank. Every fiber, nerve and molecule within me wanted you instantly."

"You're so silly," she giggled.

"There's nothing silly about my feelings for you, or—"

"Or what?" she cut me off mid-sentence.

"Or how much I want to be with you," I said.

She smiled and looked at me with her greyish blue eyes and said,

"If only that were true."

Her dismissiveness of my feelings only made me want her more. Deliberately making herself emotionally unavailable and playing hard to get made me excited in every way. It forced me to want to prove my interest in her. Social media dating and the plethora of thirsty women I hooked up with made me forget how fun the chase was. The art of the chase involves mutual respect and fun courtship rather than playing games and creating unnecessary obstacles on purpose. Men will always chase a confident woman. Jen was confident and alluring. It excited me. She excited me.

Nearly ten minutes of silence passed with us locked in an embrace. Her hands stroked my back, causing the towel I had wrapped around my waist to rise in the front.

She stepped back and said,

"Well hello," speaking to my prominent erection.

She spent a moment appreciating my girth as I noticed how heart-stoppingly gorgeous she was. She was in shape, small and petite. Her Baby Phat all black jumpsuit accentuated her small athletic frame. Her breasts bulged nicely against the cloth of her jacket, and her rich but understated perfume almost turned my knees to water.

"You look magnificent," I said.

She glanced down at my crotch. "And you look delicious."

I pulled her close to me, inhaling the freshness of her hair. I then pulled back just enough to lean in and kiss her soft lips. My member moved from semi firm to fully erect. She felt my reaction and pushed her pelvis firmly against me. I reached down, grabbing her ass and pulling her even harder against my erection as our lips continued to find each other. I couldn't believe how soft and delicate she felt in my arms.

"I could stay like this forever," she said in a voice just above a whisper.

We sat down on the edge of the bed as my warm hands made their way up her thighs, reaching a place of total wetness. Jen bit her lower lip, trying to stifle her moan. I was mildly surprised when I noticed she didn't have any panties on but appreciated it immensely, nevertheless. She was dripping wet and my hands slowly caressed her lovely wetness. I licked one finger and used it to circle and slowly rub her clit. Two fingers then slowly made their way into her tight sweet spot, slowly pushing through to the knuckle. I explored her wetness with soft gentle strokes, slowly reaching different areas inside of her. Jen, unable to take the pleasure, laid back, resting her head against one of the feathered pillows. I pulled out my fingers coated with her wetness. As she stared at me, I put one finger in my mouth, tasting her juices. My erection became unbearable as she sat up and pulled my other finger into her mouth.

"I want you so bad," I whispered.

Jen nodded in response. We came together in a deep kiss, grabbing on to each other as I laid on the bed. My hand was holding the back of her neck and hers held on to the side of my face. My free hand caressed its way from her neck, down her shoulders, and came to stop at her breasts. Hers unzipped my pants, taking my solid erection into her tiny hands and slowly stroking. I reached inside her top and felt her firm, perfectly proportioned breasts. I caressed them, running my fingers over them, squeezing and rubbing. Her touch, her smell and her taste sent currents of passion, lust and desire through my entire body.

Just then, Jen pushed me back, focusing her attention on my exposed member. She lowered her head, planting small kisses on the tip. I shuddered and whispered, "Damn," as I felt her warm tongue on my shaft. No girl had ever made me feel this good this fast before. No woman had ever made me want to give up all my bullshit. I laid back as she pulled my bulge deep into her mouth. Her saliva coated me, saturating my testicles. I laid there moaning in pleasure until my explosion filled her mouth. My body tensed then went limp. I wanted to reciprocate the pleasure. I summoned up the strength to part her legs and slowly went down on my knees. I opened her legs and slowly kissed the insides of her knee. Seeing her well-manicured vagina made me want to dive in. I restrained myself.

Slowly, I kissed her thighs, licking and giving small innocent bites. Before plunging my tongue inside her honey-pot, I deeply inhaled her scent. I absolutely loved it. She shuddered with anticipation.

I tasted her wetness directly which was simply divine. I varied between licking her clit, her inner and outer lips, slowly nibbling them. She willfully opened her legs wider, ready to receive my plunging tongue. I thrusted my tip deep inside her. Jen moaned loudly, clutching at my bald head. I focused my attention on making her climax. She arched her back as she gave way to a tense orgasm.

"Baby, I need you in me right now," she cried out to me, dragging me up.

We made love slowly and passionately for what seemed like hours. Exhausted, she laid in my arms as we both drifted to sleep.

*Later t*hat night, I felt the gentle touch of Jen's lips on my forehead. She had to rush home to her children. Knowing that she put her children first deepened my attraction for her. I drifted in and out of sleep as I heard her shuffle to put her clothes on. She slipped out of the room quietly. The sound of the door closing startled me. I opened my eyes then turned over and floated back off to sleep.

CHAPTER FIFTEEN

I spoke to Jen a few times after she left. I felt myself changing. I didn't want to like someone that fast, but it was something amazing about her. Something that caused me to let my guard down. As the work week began, I looked forward to my Wednesday counseling session. I was optimistic that this session would end better than the last. I didn't want to be an emotional mess. I was determined not to get caught up in my feelings this time. Whatever plan I had didn't work. Dr. T had a way of luring you in and extracting your inner most pain.

I arrived at my appointment early Wednesday afternoon. I'm not sure if it was because of anticipation or just nerves. Sheepishly, I smiled at the receptionist when I walked in. I wanted to avoid any awkward exchanges, so I didn't attempt to make any small talk.

"Good afternoon, ma'am. I'm here for my appointment," I smiled, hoping to get one back, but her face stayed the same.

"Good afternoon, sir. Please take the clipboard and fill out the self-assessment. You are early for your appointment. Dr. Thomas is still in session." Her tone was brief. She was clearly very upset from our previous conversation.

I didn't want to make the moment anymore uncomfortable, so I took the clipboard without saying anything else. I sat down in a paisley colored chair and glimpsed at the receptionist looking at me. She was wearing the same flowery print muumuu style dress with an unusual color pattern. I supposed she had a closet full of dresses like this.

I thought to myself, "I'm sure it's difficult to find anything that would fit someone her size." Our eyes locked for instance, and it was as if she could read my mind. She hastily turned and closed the glass partition. I laughed, thinking about all the inappropriate fat jokes I had heard.

"Yo mama so fat, her last year's Christmas picture is still printing."

"Yo mama's New Year's resolution is to help all her friends gain ten pounds so she can look skinnier."

"You know what a fat girl and a moped have in common? They are both fun to ride until your friends see you!"

I was an asshole. Dr. T came to the door while I was amusing myself.

"Good afternoon, Dr. T," I said, handing him the clipboard.

"Good afternoon, Mr. Terrell." He extended his hand and then motioned for me to follow him.

We entered his office and I walked over to the chairs. I separated them before I sat down, making sure there was an appropriate enough space between them.

"How have you been since the last session, Mr. Terrell?" he asked.

"You can just call me Terrell, no need for Mr. I have been great. I met a young lady and she's awesome," I replied with a huge smile.

"Interesting," he said. He had a hue of disapproval in his tone.

"Interesting?" I replied.

"Do you think you should pursue a new relationship while you are in therapy?" he asked.

The question infuriated me. This skinny, pompous jackass quack was asking if I should be in a relationship. "Hey, look Doc, the only reason I'm here is because my Momma suggested it. I don't need this shit. I don't need no head doctor telling me about love. I got this shit. Tell me about the shit that I ask you about." My voice elevated as I responded to Dr. T. His expression, however, remained calm and unchanging. I found his expressionless demeanor a bit unnerving.

He calmly said, "Terrell, I don't have a panic button in

this room for a reason." My mind wandered. I briefly imagined his long arms jabbing me at a distance that was too far for me to connect with him. That thought quickly turned to the idea of him kicking me with legs longer than my entire upper torso. With the image of me getting my ass kicked playing in my head, I quickly calmed down.

"I apologize, sir," I said.

"Terrell, my job is not to tell you what to do but to help you see the entire picture. If you think you are ready for a relationship, then that is your choice...but have you ever heard the saying, 'hurt people, hurt people'? Well, you are a broken individual, hurt from years of pain, abuse, mistrust, dishonesty and sadness. I was simply asking, do you think it is wise to invite someone into your life before you have dealt with those issues?" His question made sense. I hadn't loved anyone in a long time. Hell, I wasn't sure how to love anyone. The last thing I wanted to do was hurt Jen.

"You have given me a lot to think about, Dr. T," I said.

"That's why I am here. The last time we spoke, you talked about your relationship with your step dad. Can we start back there?" he asked, changing the subject.

"Sure," I said.

"You said that your step dad ruled the house with intimidation and rage," he stated.

"Yes, my step dad had his own set of rules. I remember one midsummer afternoon, I was on the couch watching TV when I heard someone unlock the front door. Momma was working her usual shift at the library and wouldn't be back for hours. I figured my Dad had the same schedule. But when he came through the door, I realized I was wrong."

"Hey Dad, how's it going?" I asked.

It was rare that he was home at that time of day.

"It's about time I talk to you and the rest of these kids," he replied, shouldering past me to the kitchen. He came back a few seconds later with a cold beer and grabbed the TV remote that I'd left on the couch.

"There are gonna be days when your mom and I get back from work and are gonna want some alone time. I ain't gonna want a bunch of kids around, that's why you got a bedroom." He paused to drink some beer. "I expect you to use it."

I knew the apartment was in Momma's name and I was frustrated because we had lost the house we had in Eastwood Acres. Before I could catch myself or think about what I was about to say, I blurted out,

"My Momma pays the rent here, not you, so this is my house too." As soon as the words fell from my lips, I knew I was in trouble.

Harry snapped. He slammed down his beer and leapt out of his chair, grabbing me by the neck. I was about five feet tall at the time and Harry was a foot and some inches taller than me. When he picked me up by my neck, my head almost touched the ceiling. My step dad's arms were huge. The few seconds he held me up seemed like an eternity. I was helpless, and I couldn't breathe. I wanted to scream, "Get your hands off me," but I couldn't. I couldn't speak at all and I felt like the life was slowly leaving my body.

"Don't you ever talk back to me," he growled. "And if you don't get out of my sight, you're gonna wish you never met me." He shoved me against the wall and dropped me. I ran away from him as fast as I could. Without a word, I raced up the stairs to my room. My brothers were quiet, afraid to make any sounds. I laid across the bottom bunk, thinking about what had just happened.

"Terrell!" Harry was calling me back downstairs. Thirty minutes had passed and as I walked down stairs, I could see he was starting on his second six pack. He stood there holding a black leather strap.

"You think you are a man now huh?" he asked.

"No, sir," I said, fearing what was about to happen.

"Yes, you do. Hold out your hand," he said.

My brothers and I had been in foster care and I stood there as he swung wildly. Each chop blistering my hands and causing discoloration. My hand, arm and fingers began to swell. He wanted to draw blood and he did. When I couldn't bear the pain any longer, I jerked my hands away, causing him to swing and hit himself. He became enraged, reeling the strap without any aim, seeking only to strike some part of my body. My only defense was to ball up in the corner and hope that he tired soon. I stayed in that fetal position until he was exhausted. Panting and dripping with sweat, he sent me to my room. I could barely move. Welts covered my face, back and arms. I couldn't cry. The shock of what just happened petrified me. I went back to my bottom bunk and laid down. I couldn't understand why he hated me so much. I couldn't understand how he could beat me so mercilessly.

About an hour later, I heard the front door slam. I looked out my room window and saw my step dad get in his 88 T Top Monte Carlo SS.

"Did you tell your mom?" Dr. T questioned, bringing me back to reality.

"No, I didn't."

"How is it that she didn't notice?" he asked.

"Momma worked two jobs. When she got off her first job we were still at school, and when she came home from her second job we were in bed, and when we got up for school she was asleep. It was a slew of circumstances that kept us revolving around each other without noticing each other."

"Are you the only one your step dad directed his anger towards?"

"No, all of my brothers had their moments. After my step dad left, my oldest brother went downstairs to get me some ice and Vaseline. He was halfway back up the stairs when the front door opened. It was Harry carrying a Budweiser twelve-pack. My brother tried to get up the steps before my step dad came in, but he wasn't fast enough."

"What are you doing down here?" My step dad's voice boomed through the living room and his face twisted with anger.

Trembling, Ron, my oldest brother, said,

"Terrell is bleeding and I wanted to get him some ice and Vaseline." His voice shook as he talked, not wanting to ignite Harry's wrath.

"I'm going back to my room now," he said, slowly moving back up the stairs. Harry put the twelve pack down and began walking up behind him. He lunged for him, grabbing the back of Ron's shirt.

"When I want you upstairs, you stay upstairs," he yelled.

"But I..." Ron stammered.

"But I nothing." *WHAP!* Harry cuffed him hard in the jaw with the back of his hand. The impact snapped his head back, splitting his lip. I could see the blood trickle down the corner of his mouth as he stumbled back into the room. As Ron came into the room, Harry kicked him. His heavy black work boot slammed against his leg, causing him to spill forward onto his face.

"Stop, please." I yelled to no avail.

"You want some more?" he asked briefly, turning his attention to me. I couldn't believe this nightmare. Harry kept coming towards Ron. Somehow, he ducked underneath Harry's flailing arms and sprinted into the hallway bathroom.

"Open up or I will knock it down!" he yelled. I heard him crash his full body weight into the bathroom door. The soft frame began to split and crack. Ron had no choice but to open it up. Harry stood there, his eyes blazing like a madman with clenched fists. Ron had nowhere to run to and no idea what to do. I peered out the door and saw him backing away from Harry.

He tripped and fell backward into the tub. My step dad stepped forward, placing one foot into the tub just inches from Ron's face. I remember thinking if he kicked him, he would break his nose or worse. I never felt so helpless. I squinted, waiting for Harry's next move. Instead of hitting him, he just stood over him, glaring at him as Ron basked in his fear.

"Don't you ever come down after I tell you to stay upstairs. Do you hear me?" He nudged my brother's shoulder with his thick square toe of his boot.

"I hear you," Ron said. His voice quaked just above a whisper. Harry walked back downstairs, reminding us that this was his house.

Dr. T quietly handed me a box of Kleenex. "I'm sorry that you had to experience that abuse." I didn't realize I was crying again. I reached for the tissues and wiped my eyes.

"I'm curious, Terrell, why didn't you tell your mother about the abuse?" he asked.

"Dr. T, my Momma was already being beaten. If we would have told her, she would have stood up to him and he would have killed her. I was scared. I was scared all the time. Fear ruled my life...so much so that I couldn't function in school. My self-esteem was low, and I didn't think I deserve anything good. I used to look at the other kids with jealousy. They were all so confident. They all had someone backing them. I went home to a step dad that called me stupid or dumb or sorry. Then I joined a church with a pastor that was just as abusive, calling us sorry or broke or stupid. Then I married a woman that used the same language. I didn't think I deserved anything better." I could feel the tears flowing. My heart hurt thinking about that kid starving for fatherly reassurance. All my life I just wanted someone in my corner. Someone that believed I was great. I had been laughed at, teased and put down so long I doubted my own validity. As I sat there with my head in my hands, Dr. T. handed me the box again. He waited until I composed myself before he spoke.

"Do you mind if I share a story with you?"

"Not at all," I said.

"I remember being a newlywed trying to figure out how to help my wife. I was in school not making much money and she carried the load. I was taught that a man takes care of his family, so I felt like shit. My wife would offer advice and solutions with such good intentions. Finally, I stopped her and said, 'This is what I need to hear: Just tell me I'm going to be okay.' Sometimes we just need reassurance. Have you ever heard of words of affirmation?"

"No, I can't say I have. What is that?" I asked.

"Words spoken at the right time are like gold apples in silver settings. That's not my quote, that's a proverb." He said, "Terrell, you have the power to change someone's day and outlook on life or your own day and outlook simply by offering encouraging words that lift the spirit. Sometimes you must encourage yourself. So, every day I wake up, I look in the mirror and say one of the following. Or sometimes I say all that apply." He handed me a pamphlet titled, *"Words of Affirmation."* I glanced through the 19 quotes.

1. I am superior to negative thoughts and low actions.
2. I have been given endless talents which I begin to utilize today.
3. I forgive those who have harmed me in my past and peacefully detach from them.
4. I am guided in my every step by the Spirit who leads me towards the right thing to do.
5. I possess the qualities needed to be extremely successful.
6. My business is growing, expanding, and thriving.
7. Happiness is a choice. I base my happiness on my own accomplishments and the blessings I've been given.
8. My ability to conquer my challenges is limitless; my potential to succeed is infinite.
9. I am courageous, and I stand up for myself.
10. Today, I abandon my old habits and take up new, more positive ones.
11. I acknowledge my own self-worth; my confidence is soaring.

12. Everything that is happening now is happening for my ultimate good.

13. I am a powerhouse; I am indestructible.

14. My obstacles are moving out of my way; my path is carved towards greatness.

15. I wake up today with strength in my heart and clarity in my mind.

16. My fears of tomorrow are simply melting away.

17. I am at peace with all that has happened, is happening, and will happen.

18. My nature is Divine; I am a spiritual being.

19. My life is just beginning.

"Thank you. I will use these." I wasn't being my normal facetious self. I meant it.

"Please do, Terrell. You can utilize any of these affirmations alone or create your own unique combination based on your personal wishes and needs. What is most important is to establish a profound communication with the universe, so say it with conviction, say it in your own unique voice, and make it happen in the real world."

"I will, Dr. T."

"We have gone over our time for today. How does next Wednesday at four sound?"

"I'm good with that, Dr. T." He handed me an appointment slip and shook my hand as I walked out of his office. My red eyes warranted a little compassion from the receptionist.

She smiled and said, "See you next week," which was a vast improvement over her normal reactions.

I called Momma while driving back to base.

"Hey, Ma."

"Hey, Terrell," she said with enthusiasm in her voice.

"Ma, I saw the therapist again today."

"How did it go?"

"Ma it was draining. I talked a lot about Dad again."

She asked, "Do you want to talk about it? You don't have to."

"I don't mind. Dr. T and I talked about the abuse and the fear. The subject stayed on Harry."

"Terrell, I am so sorry." I stopped her before should could continue.

"Momma, it wasn't your fault. Harry was a bully...he was an angry man."

She said, "I know. I wish I had protected you all more."

"I know, Ma, but Dr. T is really helping me get past it."

"Is he?" she asked.

"Yes, ma'am."

"Well that's good, Terrell. I want the best for you."

I smiled. "I know, Ma. Everything is going to work out. I'm going to keep seeing Dr. T. I'm going to figure this out."

"That's good, Terrell. I love you."

"I love you too, Ma."

She hung up the phone as I pulled up to the barracks. I walked into my room and laid down. I couldn't help but reflect on the earlier session. I felt tears roll across my ear lobes as I lie on my back looking up. I began to talk to God out loud.

"*God, thank you for today. Thank you for allowing me to be used by you. I don't talk to you that often. I know you are there, I just don't know what to say. Have I disappointed you? Have I hurt you? Am I still your child? I don't know the answer to any of these questions. I do know that I love you. God I am still so angry. Why didn't you stop the beatings? Why didn't you help us? I need help, Lord. I need your help please. Teach me how to love again. Teach me how to hope again. Teach me how to live for you again. Thank you. Amen.*"

I pulled out the pamphlet of affirmations. My eyes rested on *"My life is just beginning."* I closed my eyes and went to sleep.

CHAPTER SIXTEEN

I hadn't seen Jen since that weekend. Both of our schedules were extremely busy. Jen was a Human Resources Specialist or 42A, which was a very busy job in the military. She handled the paperwork much the way an executive administrative specialist would do. I wanted to see her again. She was heavily on my mind the minute I awoke the next day. I sent her an early morning text.

Me: Good morning. R U up?

Jen: No, it's early

Me: You're in the Army, why are you still in bed.

Jen: I like my bed

Me: Can I come join you

Jen: Sure

Her quick one-word response made me pause.

Me: Did you say okay?

Jen: Dude what the hell? I said yes are you coming or not?

Me: Yes, I'm on my way.

Jen: Do you still have my address

Me: Yes

Jen: Well hurry the hell up, I don't have all day...

I laughed at her smiley face. I loved her bluntness and her sarcasm. I walked out and started my car, thinking about how much different Jen was from any other woman I had ever met. My mind drifted to her confidence and strength. She was outspoken with a sharp tongue. I not only saw her as an incredibly beautiful person in general, but I genuinely respected her as she was kind, loving, supportive and understanding. I could honestly see myself marrying her. The thought of settling down again disgusted me. I hated my ex-wife. Jen was the complete opposite, though. She was hard working and settled. She was educated and faithful. She wanted something out of life. She wanted to make something of herself. Her beauty mixed with her attributes made me think of things that I thought I had put behind me. LOVE!

Because of Tanya, I hated love! Love leaves you in the darkness, crying your eyes out. I wanted to believe in love again. But I was afraid, scared that I would experience that feeling of stupidity again. I wanted love, but I hated how much power it had over the people infected with it. I hated how much people would hurt themselves and others over it, how many horrific, unforgivable, degrading, destructive acts we commit for love. We act stupid when we're swept up in it, and it always hurts when that love is broken. I hated how much power over me it gives another person. I hated how much expectation it creates even if it's not reciprocated. I hated how disgustingly fragile love was. I hated what love makes you believe, and how it makes you open up and let people in. I hated love...but I still wanted it. I wanted it with Jen.

I was on autopilot as I pulled into the driveway of the on-post housing where Jen lived. She opened the door with anticipation as I got out of my car. My heart raced. I was still in awe of a woman as attractive as she actually wanting me. My confidence was shot from my marriage. I had physically changed but deep down I was still the remnant of a broken, 300 pound, low self-esteem, church deacon. I was a different person on the outside but the same person inside.

Jen was gorgeous, standing in the doorway of her apartment with the television news blaring behind her. I walked up to her and held her tight against me. I picked her up and kissed her passionately. My thick arms held her so tight, her feet dangled off the ground.

She whispered in my ear, "I can't breathe." I smiled and loosened my bear hug without letting her go. She felt good in my arms.

As I pulled back, she pulled me closer. She embraced me as I embraced her. I could feel her let her body yield to my touch. She exhaled as if she could finally breathe again.

"I'm comfortable with you," she said.

"I'm glad. I am comfortable with you," I replied.

"That's not something that is easy for me to do," she said.

"Why?"

"Because comfort comes with trust and trust is not something to do easily," she said.

I listened closely as she began to tell me of her messy divorce. Her ex was a cheater. It didn't make her bitter towards men but cautious and more aware of red flags. She had been single for about a year and half. It had been two years since she discovered her husband was having an affair with one of his clients. She knew the girl her husband was sleeping with and confronted her. Initially, her husband, Gary, and his mistress, Tara, both refused to acknowledge it was an affair because they had not slept together. They had had numerous meetings, phone calls and exchanged on average 40 text messages a day. Jen knew her husband. She knew his characteristics and she usually followed her intuition. Against her better judgement, she gave her husband the benefit of the doubt. Mistakenly, Gary left his email open one day and she read some of the exchanges between him and Tara. Her heart sank when she read that he loved her, and he wanted to sleep with her. She was absolutely devastated to discover the affair was real. They made her look like a paranoid fool, like someone who was making up the affair in her mind. She had so many other things on her mind at the time. She felt betrayed by him, which made her cautious with her heart.

When she confronted him about the emails, he told her he hated how she looked. She spent hours trying to make herself "look nice" so he was not embarrassed being with her. When she asked him why he had to have an affair, he said he was craving attention and that she wasn't there for him. It hurt her, but it didn't break her. She knew it was just a pathetic excuse for him to do what he wanted to do. The very next day, she left his ass. I listened intently as she told me her story.

She relaxed in my arms. I looked into her eyes and asked, "What was that?"

She asked, "Am I safe?"

I sat up, setting my feet on the floor. My eyes met her gaze. I knew what she wanted to hear but I also knew myself. I was somber and searching. I wanted to be what she wanted. I wanted to be who she was asking me to be, but I didn't know if I could. Her vulnerability made me want to try. I knew that being vulnerable wasn't easy for her. If she was willing to let her guard down, I could try to be a better man. I tucked her hair back behind her ears.

"Jen, I will not purposely hurt your heart. I am not a perfect man. I have flaws. Many, many flaws," I said.

She looked at me and said, "Don't hurt me."

Before she could say another word, I cupped her face in my hands and covered her mouth with mine. For a moment, time stood still as my soft lips pressed against hers. She could feel my kiss growing hungry and possessive. My tongue thrust into her mouth, flicking against hers, and every thought of pushing me away fled as something else took hold of her. Something she hadn't allowed herself to feel but could no longer deny. She was falling in love. Suddenly, she noticed the heart that went along with the man. She appreciated me. She appreciated my physique. Every inch of me was solid muscle. She'd hugged me before. Hell, she'd seen me in my underwear before. But this time, this day, she looked at me differently. Now the feeling of all those muscles pressed against her set fire to her insides. She ran her fingertips across my solid chest and broad shoulders and then down to my lean washboard abs. The press of my body against hers did things to her insides she hadn't felt in a longtime. I was rock behind the zipper of my jeans, and my thick erection throbbed against her stomach.

A quiet moan left her throat. Her body sagged into mine. Her arms wound themselves tighter around my neck, drawing me closer as she lifted onto her toes to deepen the contact. I sensed her surrender as my hands released her face. My arms came around her body again. I let out a quiet, relieved groan that sounded torn from his chest. My body trembled against hers and for a moment, we clung to each other as our kiss softened to something more tender, more achy and needy. My lips moved down her neck, sending goose bumps skittering across the surface of her skin. Her heart pounded. Her blood rushed in her ears. Her world felt as if it had tipped on its axis. It had never been this way with anyone. At least, that's what she'd told me later.

All I could think about was how much I needed her right then. Something shifted between us and our feelings were changing. The invisible band keeping us guarded snapped. Hands flew everywhere, shoving clothing out of the way. I pushed her t-shirt up her chest and bent my head. My hot mouth latched onto her puckered, aching nipples.

Her hands moved to the button on my jeans. She yanked it open, taking the zipper with it, and reached inside to stroke my full erection. I groaned as I moved my hands to the waistband of her jeans. I undid the button and slid down the zipper. She released her firm grasp of my member long enough to wiggle her pants down her hips. As she kicked them away, my gaze caught hers. Something hot and tangible moved between us. A silent acknowledgement. I reached down and lifted her. She wrapped her legs around my hips. Her back hit the wall behind her as my mouth crashed down on hers.

Our bodies shook as I entered her. She closed her eyes and held on tight, her fingers clutching me close. Her soft moans excited me more. I wanted to match her moans with loving words but all I could say was "Oh shit." My whole body tensed as my explosion filled her. We fell onto the couch with me still inside her. I slowly stroked her until my semi firm erection was stiff again. I began vigorously pushing myself into her over and over. A fierce, desperate rhythm that made her body quiver and produce thick creamy juices. Her nails curled into my back. I dropped my head into the curve of her neck as we climaxed together. We laid motionless. How long we remained that way, I don't know. Long moments passed as we simply clung to each other in the aftermath of something more powerful than either of us had experienced.

I was the first to move, rolling over onto my side and pulling her close to me. Our exchange hadn't been about sex. It had been...something phenomenal. A connection of minds and souls, beyond the body. Never in a million years did I think I would find that with her. The way she stared at me echoed the same acknowledgment. I stroked her face with my fingers, soft and tender, and smiled that familiar dimpled grin that she could only now admit made her stomach do somersaults.

I pressed my lips against her forehead and whispered,

"I can't hold back anymore. I want to love you the way you need to be loved."

Tears streamed down her face, an unstoppable river as the truth flowed over her and through her. It was as if the knowledge had always been there, all along, waiting for her to see it.

She pressed her mouth to my mouth, whispering against my lips, "I love you, Terrell." Hearing those words and feeling the truth behind them lifted a weight. I felt what she said. I felt her heart and I loved her too. This was real for me. This was true to me. She was my first love. She helped me feel something I hadn't felt in a long time...happiness!

Jen and I spent the next few days together. We had that sickening, budding relationship behavior. The kind that makes you want to be around each other all the time and tell each other everything. I told Jen about my therapy. She was supportive and when Wednesday came, she reminded me about my afternoon appointment.

I arrived at the appointment early as usual. I was eager to tell Dr. T about my new-found love. Awkwardly, I smiled at the receptionist when I walked in. I had resolved that the exchange between us wasn't going to change. I wanted to avoid any awkward conversations, so I didn't attempt to make any small talk.

"Good afternoon, ma'am," I smiled, knowing her face would stay the same.

"Good afternoon, sir. Please take the clipboard and fill out the self-assessment. You are early, and Dr. Thomas is still in session." Her tone was brief as always.

She was noticeably still very upset from our prior conversation. I took the clipboard without saying anything else. I sat down and filled out my paperwork. Dr. T came to the door while I was writing.

"Good afternoon, Dr. T," I said, handing him the clipboard.

"Good afternoon, Mr. Terrell." He extended his hand and then motioned for me to follow him.

I walked in and before I sat down in my usual spot, I adjusted the chairs. Dr. T never said anything about my idiosyncrasy. He knew that everyone had a mode of behavior or way of thought that seemed peculiar to everyone except that individual. I liked Dr. T. He was a simple man. He kept his office the same exact way. I don't know if it was to give a sense of normalcy or if he just hated change. I could tell that he liked having everything remain in the same place. Perfection was his idiosyncrasy. I didn't mind because I hated change too. He sat down and crossed his long legs, exposing his black and white argyle socks.

"Mr. Terrell, how are you today?"

"I'm great."

"Great?" he asked. "What has you in such a high-spirited mood?"

"Well, I think I'm in love," I said with a huge smile on my face.

Dr. T's stoic look allowed me to know I would not be pleased with his next question. He leaned back in his chair and asked, "Are you sure you are ready for love...or even a relationship?"

I could feel my expression change and I think he noticed my facial expression. He quickly diffused my growing frustration with another question.

"Why did you get divorced?" The question silenced me for a moment.

He then asked, "Do you think you are over her?" He

paused. "Let me rephrase the question. Are you over your anger for her?" he asked.

Quietly, I said, "I am not angry at her. I hate her."

"Hate," he said, "is one of those negative emotions that rarely does any good. More often, it festers in us, causing us to obsess over the matter. It wastes your time, energy, and talent. It dominates your life, stealing your focus away from improving yourself. And every second that you indulge in loathing another person is a step backwards in your pursuit of happiness. Instead of advancing toward your goals, this intense emotion puts you on a destructive detour and it keeps you from truly moving forward. So how can you wholeheartedly love someone if you haven't dealt with the hate for someone else?"

I knew he was right, but I didn't want to hear him. I knew he was going to tell me that I shouldn't be with Jen until I let my anger go. I knew he was going to tell me what my Mamma would say, "Don't open that door until you close the other." I didn't want to hear it. I was over Tanya. I didn't love her, and I never did. My dislike for her had steadily grown into hatred. My stomach turned at the thought of talking to her.

"Why did you and your ex divorce?" he asked.

I took a deep breath and sighed. "I could live with her bouncing checks all over South Carolina. I could live with her lying to the church. I could even live with her bad mouthing me around town. Tanya was a piss poor mother and a piss poor homemaker. None of that mattered to me. I can cook, I can clean for myself, so none of that bothered me. What affected me was I caught my wife cheating and stealing from my kids. She put on such a good act. She fooled me. The very thing that she had accused me of, the very thing that she said I was doing, she did. She cried in church, laid out at the altar purging and crying, stood in the prayer lines, and the entire time her fake ass was cheating and stealing. She's a lying, crooked, no good hypocretin ass BITCH!" I paused for a moment to calm down. After gaining my composure, I continued.

"Dr. T, I'm going to share something with you that I have never told anyone. Before me and my ex broke up, we tried to fix things. She never worked, but in an effort to fix things, she found a job. This was one of the major issues that caused problems in our marriage. Finding out she was employed gave me a glimmer of hope that she was changing. Tanya told me that she had a job at a department store, I think the name was Peebles. Anyway, she always had to work the evening shift, so I would watch the children. I didn't mind. I thought it was because she wanted to make up for the money we lost, but after work she would say she was going to her parent's house. Her parents were elderly, and I loved them. I understood. I didn't mind in the beginning when she first got the job, but after a while it pissed me off. She had been working about four weeks and she hadn't received a check yet. I understood that they held the first two weeks but by the third or fourth week some money should have been coming. So finally, after five weeks of working and no money to show, I told her that I didn't want my wife out all hours of the night working for nothing. She lied and said she donated her first check to Pastor Prangles. I actually believed that lie because I knew Prangles was money hungry and greedy. Then she went into the pathetic crying spell, accusing me of not trusting her. So, I let it go for a while. By the time week six rolled around, I was fed up. When she went to work on that Friday evening, I borrowed my brother's car and went to her parent's house with the children. While there, I got a call from Tanya saying she was off from work and going to their house. I said okay, never acknowledging that I was there."

"The town we were in was so small, it didn't take long to spot the car she was in. It was her parents white Honda. She went to the only restaurant in town with Lawrence. I know this sounds crazy, but I waited and then I followed them after they left. While following them, I got caught at a light and lost them. After driving for a while, I found the car. She was sneaky and parked the car in the church parking lot. OUR CHURCH! I had no idea where they were at. So, I patiently waited. The church was large and had a lot of places to hide. I hid and after about an hour they came walking down the street holding hands and laughing. They sat back in the car for about thirty minutes. Her head was in his lap. When they got out, I saw the guy adjusting his pants. Naturally, thirty minutes in a car with her head in his lap and the guy adjusting himself reeked of a blowjob. Let me tell you, that hurts worse than just sex. Obviously, sex is bad enough, but sucking this guy off in the church yard is even worse. She was pleasuring him, and to what end? I remember thinking, What is she getting out of that? I felt my soul turn into ice. Then they left and walked down the street. I stealthily followed behind them and waited till they went into the house. I didn't know it at the time, but this guy lived about 100 yards from the church. Why would they park at the church and not his house? Obviously because she sorely underestimated me? I don't know exactly what she was thinking, I can only guess that she DID think I might follow them, but if all I found was her car, I still wouldn't know where she was."

Dr. T listened quietly. As I paused, he said, "I understand why you are angry and feel betrayed."

I interrupted. "No, sir, you don't understand."

"What is it you're not telling me, Terrell?"

I took a deep breath. "I knew she was cheating. I knew it the entire time. I chose to believe something else."

Dr. T listened to my pain. "How did you know?"

"Because the day before all this happened, my car got repossessed. When that happened, I called the bank and they told me I had a warrant for my arrest because my account was 500 dollars in the negative. I went to the bank and they showed me photos and a video feed of the people accessing my account. It was Tanya and her new fucking friend. It's ALL because of that CHURCH! I sat there like a FOOL having faith! Here I was believing what I was taught. I held on to what I believed instead of what I knew. I overlooked my own common sense."

Dr. T interrupted me. "Terrell, who are you really angry with?"

"What do you mean?"

"You say you are angry at your ex. And you are extremely bitter about the things she has done. You have a lot of anger. But I suspect that a lot of this anger is at yourself."

"Myself?"

"Yes, Terrell," Dr. T continued. "Yourself. Listen, anger is a natural and mostly automatic response to pain in one form or another, physical or emotional. We get angry when we feel rejected, feel threatened, or experience some loss. Anger is a substitute emotion. By this, I mean that sometimes people make themselves angry so that they don't have to feel pain. People change their feelings of pain into anger because it feels better to be angry than it does to be in pain. You are angry, Terrell. You are angry with cause. Often when you are angry with a cause you feel that the people who have hurt me are wrong and they should be punished. Do you want to harm your ex-wife or Pastor Prangles? Do you think hurting them will bring you satisfaction?"

The stare between Dr. T and I seemed like it lasted for hours. It was a quiet stare. I knew the answer to his question and so did he. Not a day passed that I didn't think about murdering one of those two. NOT ONE DAY! I wanted them both to die a slow painful death. I wanted to watch. I wanted to cause it. The only hesitation I had about killing Tanya was that it would hurt my children. Outside of that, I didn't care. I wanted to set her on fire and watch her burn. I wanted to tie her to the back of my car and drive faster than she could run. I wanted to make her run until her feet blistered and drag her after her legs gave out from exhaustion.

I wanted to walk up to the pulpit in the middle of church service, pull out my nine-millimeter and shoot Prangles in the chest. I wanted to watch him gasp from his sucking chest wound. I wanted to stand over him and watch the confused, questioning look of *why* on his face. I wanted to see his expression as every lie, every twisted scripture, every manipulated 'word from God' came back to his mind. I wanted to smile as he died. I looked at Dr. T thinking YES... Yes, I want to harm them. But I knew better than to say it out loud.

"No, Dr. T. I don't wish harm on no man. I have to go, Dr. T."

"Are you sure?"

"Yes," I said abruptly.

"Well these are your sessions and if you want to end it early, I can't force you to stay. I would like to see you tomorrow, Terrell. Do you think that's possible?"

"No, Dr. T, I don't think that's possible."

I was tired of his psychoanalytical babble. I didn't want to hear any more of his bullshit. This crap wasn't helping me anyway, I thought. Fuck this!

"Well, I have a few open sessions next week, Terrell. Do you want to make an appointment?"

"No, Dr. T. I don't!"

Dr. T's patient expression never changed. He knew I was angry. The session had been hard. He was a seasoned counselor. He had seen my reaction many times. He knew not to push.

"As I stated earlier, I have a few open sessions next week, Terrell. I will keep tomorrow at three open and our regular time next week. Today was not a bad day, even though it was difficult. I really would like to see you tomorrow."

I remained silent. When he was done talking, I walked out without speaking. The receptionist motioned for me to come to the counter, but I walked past. I wasn't in the mood for her fat ass sarcasm. Anger was an emotion I was comfortable with. I had been angry for so long, it wasn't a second emotion. It was my primary emotion. I sat in my car and turned on my phone. I had voice messages from several missed calls. I wasn't in the mood to talk or to listen to anyone. I just wanted to go home and sleep.

On my way home, I stopped by the liquor store. I was in the mood for some Crown and I didn't want to share. I wanted to drink uninterrupted and decided to turn my phone off. As soon as I touched it, it rang. "Who the fuck is this?" I said out loud. It was an unknown number.

"Hello?"

"Is this Deacon Terrell?"

A chill and anger came over my body. I hadn't been called Deacon in almost two years.

"Who the hell is this?" I asked.

"Whoa, slow your roll man. What's with all the hostility? Terrell, this is Jamie."

Jamie was one of the up and coming ministers at the church. When I left Trueway Church, he was the new flavor of the month, a young minister that Pastor Prangles routinely paraded in front of us as if he was special. He was dumb. And Prangles used his stupidity. Jamie always wanted to impress Prangles, so he would come and work at the Church for free, always building something or fixing something on Saturdays. Every Saturday! And on Sunday, Pastor Prangles would tell us how much better than all of us he was because his dumb ass worked for free on a Saturday while the rest of us went to our regular jobs. Fuck him...I couldn't stand him then and today ain't the day for no fucking reunion.

"How the fuck you got my number?"

"Bruh, slow down. I know you ain't at Trueway Church no more. I ain't either."

"Okay, good for you. Now what do you want?" I was short and to the point. I didn't care if I was a member or not. I didn't like his ass.

"I have been asking around and everybody told me that you might be able to answer some questions for me."

"What questions?" Obviously agitated, I sharply said,

"Dude, get to the fucking point. Do I sound like I'm in the mood to talk?"

"Okay, okay, bruh. Calm down. They told me your temper was bad, Jesus. Okay listen, the other day one of the members found some old letters. The letters were from Pastor Prangles to Missionary Gilson. They were screwing around." He started laughing. "The whole-time Pastor was blasting you from across the pulpit, he was doing the same thing."

Quietly, I asked, "What did you say?"

"All those trips to Aiken and Williston, all those nights he came to church late or arrived in a separate car from First Lady Prangles, he was out cheating." I could hear him laughing. I hung up the phone. Jamie called back a few times, but I turned off my phone. I drove back to my place in silence. I walked in, sat on the couch and opened up my bottle of Crown. I didn't need a cup or glass. I took a sip and thought about the day. I took a bigger swallow and reclined my chair.

CHAPTER SEVENTEEN

I woke up on the couch the next day. My bottle was empty. I looked at the clock in horror. I overslept. I missed the first three hours of my shift. I turned on my phone and it blared like crazy. I called my supervisor, preparing for the ass chewing I was about to get.

Sergeant First Class Meadows wasn't big on small talk or excuses. He was a former Drill Instructor and he thought that new soldiers were weak. He said it all the time. "You new soldiers are soft as baby shit," or "I should call you Duncan Hines because you are soft as cookie dough." He was a hard, old school soldier, the kind that ran five miles and told you about it. He sang army songs and always talked like he was seconds from whipping your ass. He wasn't mean, but he was unyielding, defiant and uncompromising. He picked up after the first ring.

"Dammit, Specialist Terrell, you better be dead or close to dead or I swear before all that's holy you gonna wish you was. I don't give a gnat's ass where you are or what you are doing. You better be calling to tell me you 're walking in this goddamn building right now." The only thing I could think of was an honest lie.

"Sargent Meadows, I have been having some problems dealing with my Dad's death. I have been going to a therapist off post. Yesterday was a hard day and I had one too many. I overslept. I have another appointment today. I will be working shortly. I may have to leave early to make this appointment. I really do need help." Sargent Meadows paused, and then his next remarks shocked me.

"Terrell, I'm going to put you down as sick leave for today. You are not on the schedule for the next few days. Go get the help you need. I NEED to hear from you every day. I also need you to come in tomorrow for a counseling statement. I lost my father last year, so I know how you feel."

"Thanks, Sargent Meadows."

"Don't thank me, thank the Army."

I had no idea what he meant by that, so I just said, "Aight, I'll see you tomorrow."

"Roger that, Hooah. I'm out!"

I felt like shit. I knew my partial lie saved me from an unpleasant situation, but I played on a sore subject for someone else. I wouldn't have missed a day for my step dad, but I had to play the cards I was dealt. I had no intention of ever going back to see Dr. T but now I had too. The next call I made was to his office. His receptionist answered the phone.

"Good morning, this is a Fresh Start Mental Health Clinic. My name is Nancy, how can I help you?"

"Good morning, Ms. Nancy. This is Terrell. Dr. T set aside an appointment time for me today. I would like to confirm the time and come in."

"Sure, Terrell, I can do that for you. Just one minute. Okay, I have you in for one o'clock today."

"Thank you, Ms. Nancy."

"No problem. I will see you this afternoon."

That was the most pleasant conversation we had. I wasn't sure if she knew who I was or if she was sympathetic to my meltdown the day before. Nevertheless, it was a pleasant exchange. I set my alarm for 11:30. Jen had texted me a few times, and I imagined she called also since my voicemail was full, but I didn't want to talk to her. I didn't want to talk so I laid back down until my alarm rang.

I arrived at the appointment early. I wasn't eager to talk to Dr. T. This was just a formality. I needed a note showing I was in therapy the previous day as well as the current day. There was no awkward smile between the receptionist and me. Nothing was going to change, and I was never going to see her again.

"Good afternoon, ma'am."

"Good afternoon, sir. Please take the clipboard and fill

out the self-assessment. Dr. Thomas is still in session." Her tone was brief as always.

I took the clipboard without saying anything else. I sat down and filled out my paperwork. Twenty or thirty minutes passed before Dr. T came to the door while I was writing. Dr. T was always punctual. I imagined if he was off his schedule for a patient, he had someone in his office that was a real nut.

"Good afternoon, Mr. Terrell." He extended his hand, expecting me to shake it. Begrudgingly, I did as he motioned for me to follow him. I walked into his office and sat down in my usual spot. Dr. T. could feel the tension.

"Why are you angry, Terrell?'

I wasn't expecting this question. It wasn't the typical way he started our sessions. I took a deep breath.

"Dr. T, I know I am holding on to something I need to let go. I just don't know how."

"Terrell, that's real honesty. A part of healing is being honest with yourself."

"You asked me yesterday if I wanted to hurt Prangles and Tanya. I don't want to hurt them, but I wouldn't care if something bad happened. It wouldn't bother me at all."

"Terrell, I understand why you hold so much animosity towards your ex, but why so much anger for your former pastor?"

"Bishop Prangles was an evil man. It took me a longtime to figure it out. He is a master manipulator. The people that attend church are focused on trying to hear from God. We as church members are taught that the pastor is that doorway to God's voice. Prangles knew this. Most of our members were mothers from broken homes or married women whose husbands wanted no parts of church. We didn't have a lot of money, but we all had faith. We had faith that if we believed or prayed or shouted then the things in our lives that were broken would miraculously be fixed. All we had to do was believe!"

Dr. T interrupted me, "Terrell, I'm not an overtly religious person but isn't the essence of faith believing?"

"Yes, it is. Faith is believing. I'm not sure how I can explain this, but some small churches put a lot of emphasis on the pastor. He is not God, but he is the Man of God. After years of hearing that phrase Man of God, a narcissistic person like Prangles starts to believe he is. He becomes dominating and authoritative."

"I'm curious, Terrell. Your mother brought you all there. Why did you all stay after witnessing such ill-treatment?"

"Dr. T, this was our first real experience with church. This is all we knew. We just wanted relief from life. All we wanted to do was come to God's house on Sunday and relax in God's grace. But Prangles ruined it. He ruined the church. He developed doctrines from pet verses that supported his agenda. If he wanted a new car, he talked about giving. If he wanted you to marry somebody, he talked about Adam and Eve. If he wanted you to fear him or respect him or do what he said, he talked about Hell or servants obeying their masters. He had the ability to make people feel that they could not make important decisions or know God's will without him. People were only treated kindly when they submitted to his doctrines and authority."

I could tell Dr. T was confused. He was an educated man. It was hard for him to understand blind faith. Talking about it out loud made me feel foolish. Prangles exalted himself before the church, ridiculed everybody, took joy in making other men look small in the eyes of their families, provoked and intimidated people to get what he wanted and demanded respect instead of trying to earn respect. Yet we all still blindly followed him as a leader. He was a master manipulator.

"Terrell, is this why you have so much hate for him?"

"Yes, this is why I hate him. People go to church for a lot of reasons. I was taught that church is an act of obedience to God and it honors the Lord's Day. People need help to face the issues of life. Faith as presented through the teachings of the Bible and show how believers in the past struggled, grew and lived out their faith from different perspectives. Bishop Prangles knew those things and manipulated them to get his way. And now I know he was a liar and a cheater. One of his ministers called me yesterday. Prangles has been cheating on his wife with one of the members. All those years I sat through the most brutal, self-serving, ruthless church services. And the entire time he was cheating on his wife. My whole life has been a reaction or attempt to recover from this fucked up cult ministry." I stopped talking. I was beyond angry.

"Terrell, being hurt by someone, particularly someone you love and trust, can cause a lot of anger. You had a love for your ex-wife and your former pastor and that's why their betrayal is so difficult for you to digest. If you dwell on hurtful events or situations, grudges filled with resentment, vengeance and hostility can take root. If you allow negative feelings to crowd out positive feelings, you might find yourself swallowed up by your own bitterness or sense of injustice."

I knew he was right, but I wasn't ready to hear him. I didn't want to hear him. I didn't want to forgive or let go.

"Dr. T, maybe forgiveness will come in the future. Maybe I can stop hating them later but right now I can't."

"Terrell, the moment you let yourself be affected by hate, then you lose. Your decision-making will be affected, and you may lose control and do something that you will only regret later. Look at the choices you have made. Are you happy with who you are? You must work at regaining your self-control. Do you meditate?"

"No, I don't meditate."

"Meditation reduces stress, fosters clear thinking, and increases our capacity for empathy and compassion."

"Empathy? Compassion? I don't want to empathize with my ex and I damn sure don't want to have compassion for Prangles lying ass."

"Terrell, hate is a very destructive emotion that you

should not let yourself have. It is a pernicious emotion that can literally drain your energy. To me, it has no positive value whatsoever except in case of defending your life or property from violent attacks. It can consume your well-being and poison your mind. Know how bad the emotion of hate is and promise yourself that you will never let this emotion control any of your thinking or action."

Nothing Dr. T said made a difference. I wasn't changing my mind. The only thing I could think of while he talked was "I wonder what pernicious means." I didn't want to seem stupid so I just nodded as if I knew what he was saying. When the session was over, I thanked Dr. T. I didn't schedule another appointment. I needed a break from all this soul searching. I asked Nancy for two excuses, one for the previous day and the present. I walked out the door knowing that this was my last visit. Before I could get in my car, I heard my name being called. It was Dr. T in full stride walking across the parking lot.

"Did I forget something?'

"No, Terrell. I know you may not be attending any more sessions. I wanted to give you my card and to let you know that if in a crisis, you can call anytime."

"Thank you, Dr. T." I shook his hand, got in my car and drove off.

CHAPTER EIGHTEEN

As good as Jen had handled me in bed, sexing her hadn't done a damn thing to take my mind off my last few sessions. The revelation that Pastor Prangles was a cheater made things worse. I was conflicted...I missed Jen, but I didn't feel like being bothered. I ignored her calls. I put my head down and went to work. Sergeant First Class Meadows was looking for me every day. Because I had missed two consecutive days, I had to report to him directly. He was a hard man, but he had a way of showing concern. Every day he would ask, "You alright, Specialist?" He seemed uncomfortable showing concern. It wasn't in his nature.

I appreciated it though and always responded, "Roger, I'm good."

It was a lie. I wasn't good. I wasn't sleeping at night and

the smallest thing would set me off. I was on edge. My mind was clouded with thoughts of the Pastor. I was obsessed. I wanted to hurt him as bad as he hurt me. I battled with this obsession for a while. Days turned into weeks of going to work and then going home. Weeks of ignoring calls and being alone. Weeks of thinking about Prangles lies and long-winded, hateful sermons. It was during one of those low points I heard a knock at my door. It was Jen.

She walked right in as I opened the door. Jen greeted me with sarcasm.

"Well hello, stranger."

"Hey, Jen."

I almost lost it. She had on an incredible satin dress that accentuated her breasts and hugged her curves. She was playing a game. She thought someone else was at my house and she wanted to show that she was the baddest chick. If there was someone there, I would have put their ass out.

Jen was so damn sexy, and she greeted me with,

"You look like shit, Terrell."

I laughed. I had been so preoccupied with my hatred for Bishop Prangles, I didn't realize I wasn't shaving. I usually kept a smooth bald head, but stubble was showing. She noticed it. I loved her forward attitude. Her attitude matched mine. Neither of us had a filter and neither of us cared.

"Yes, Jen, I guess I have let myself go a little."

"Are you okay?" she asked. "I haven't heard from you and you haven't returned my calls. What's going on?"

I thought about telling her everything. I wanted to open up about the sessions. I was scared. Who wants to say, "Hey, I'm thinking about killing my ex-wife and former Pastor. I haven't called you because I have been consumed with rage and murderous thoughts." Somehow, I knew that conversation wouldn't bring us closer together. So, I told her half a story.

"Jen, I have been struggling. These last few sessions have weighed me down."

"Terrell, that's what communication is for. All you have to do is talk to me. You shut me out and don't say anything. I thought you had another chick."

I laughed. "Is that why you came over here unannounced?"

She wasn't smiling when she said, "Yes.

Look, Terrell, life is short and if you are gonna be fucking around and doing childish shit, then I ain't got time for you or your bullshit. I like you ...maybe even love you, but I love me more. So, fuck the silly shit."

I knew what she was saying, and she was right. I wasn't being the most straight forward guy. Talking to her made me feel good. I felt like I should let things go. The past was holding me back. I was on the verge of something really good and it was time to put the past aside. Jen sat down on the couch and began to make small talk.

"So, how many bitches you fucked on this couch?"

I laughed. "I had a routine that didn't allow me to bring chicks to my house."

"So, chicks let you come screw at their house or take them to hotels, but they couldn't come to your house?"

I laughed. "Yeah, something like that."

"Then why am I so special. How come I can come here?"

The question made me think. I didn't remember giving her my address. That was my rule. No one came to my house. I had always used Kisi's house. That was my fuck palace. I never wanted to have random chicks doing a pop up.

"You know, Jen, that's a good question. How did you get my address?"

She laughed. "I work in Human Resources. I can get your address, social and blood type if I want." She sat on my couch and grabbed the remote. Her confidence was so attractive. I loved how sure of herself she was. Confident women are noticeable. They stand out. They have a certain air about them that makes you want to get to know them. It makes you want to know what makes them so self-assured. They're intriguing and it's hypnotizing. They have a sense of ease which is also quite appealing. Confident women seem to know what they want and are not afraid to ask for it or go after it. Nor are they afraid to express themselves. A woman who is comfortable in her own skin and is well-adjusted stimulates a man. And Jen was arousing me.

"Don't worry, Terrell. I'm not going to just pop up. I

hadn't heard from you in a while. I wanted to make sure you were okay."

"Aww, you do care," I said jokingly.

"Yeah, I do a little bit, but don't be a bitch about it," she said, smiling and flipping through the channels.

"You were worried, is that the only reason you came?" I asked.

My body was reminding me that it had been weeks since we last had sex. I was extremely horny, and Jen was looking delicious. She looked like a devilishly tempting angel, her body hugged by the soft jersey satin of the dress, the drop of the neckline enhancing the gentle rise of her breasts. The subtle gap between her breasts only emphasizes the generous curvature of her body as the flow of her chest narrowed into her waist then flared out to her hips and lovely ass. Yet, despite how beautiful she looked, her elegant fingers pulled at the hem of her dress.

She kicked off her shoes and took down the tight bun, allowing the wildly beautiful curls of her blonde hair to cascade over her shoulders. I watched her and dear God, I wanted her. I offered her a drink and something to eat as she continued to flip channels. I glimpsed back at her while I poured her a glass of Moscato. Her clear blue eyes seemed startled as she caught me staring.

"Why are you looking at me?" she asked.

"I'm going to make love to you in that dress, Jen," I smiled, watching her visibly fight to pull her dress down past her exposed thighs.

"Oh, you think it's that easy? I ain't heard from you in weeks and you think you're just gonna get some?"

"No and yes. No, I don't think it's that easy, but yeah I think I'm gonna get me some." I laughed. My confidence wasn't lacking.

"Well, I'm afraid you are wrong." She bit her lip and looked down, smoothing her hand over the delectable curve of her hip, feeling the soft fabric which stretches over her body. "This dress is new and I'm not going to have it christened as a booty call dress. Besides, what type of woman do you think I am? It would be highly inappropriate to take part in that kind of behavior before you feed me and explain why you've been ignoring me."

"Are you teasing me, Jen? Because if you were teasing me, I would just have to show you exactly what it means to goad a man who wants you more than his next breath." I walked over to her with her wine glass. She tensed as I sat down next to her and then relaxed when my hands slid over her waist, her silken soft hair ruffled slightly by my breath as I whisper to her, "I want to feel your body next to mine." Her response instantly changed the mood.

"Who told you to sit that close to me, Terrell?" she half whispered, half murmured. She sounded somewhat annoyed and I frowned, removing my hands from her waist. Have I misread the signs? At that point, I resolved to do what I was told immediately. I slid over, giving her a little space. As I sat there, I was silent and confused. I've never in my life felt so incapable of movement than I did at that very moment. Then she stood up and walked towards me, each achingly slow step was torment and a delight. She reached her fingers to touch my face. She placed herself in my lap, her thighs on either side of mine, the hem of her dress riding up dangerously high.

"Why are you so handsome, Terrell?" she whispered as her light touch caressed my bald head. "It seems so unfair for me to have you all to myself. I do have you all to myself...right?"

Her question was suggestive. I wondered if she had heard something. Something about this situation felt wrong and right at the same time. But my erection had begun to push through my pants and my thoughts were clearly focused on one thing. "I'm yours, Jen. Do with me what you will." Before I even realized what I said, she exposed my member. A flicker of surprise echoed in her gaze as she fondled my erection, looking at it as if it was new. She rocked gently forward on my lap, placing my painfully hard erection under her skirt, outside of her panties, making me breathe in a hiss through gritted teeth.

"Stay completely still, Terrell," she whispered, her voice shaky and uncertain but her gaze steady. I nodded and waited for what seemed like an eternity as she took a breath and leaned in, kissing me briefly at first, her lips barely grazing mine, before deepening her kiss. She leaned her forehead against mine and sighs, her eyes closed as I breathed in her scent.

"I think I might have to christen this dress after all," she said softly as my hands wandered and explored her body. I slid her dress off, tossing it towards the television. Wandering slowly back down her body, my arms settle back against the chair, waiting for her next move. She adjusted and lowered herself onto me. I began nuzzling her neck, nibbling where it met her shoulder and she moaned. Her breath quickened as my nibbles turned to small bites. She slowly began grinding against my exposed erection. Her panties were wet. I could feel her moisture.

Her hands roamed down, unzipping my pants, and easing them down my waist. I pushed myself up to help slide my pants off my legs to free my aroused penis. Settling against my lap again, her hands gently scratching my chest and abs, moans escaping from her mouth at the skin to skin contact. She felt my erection swell. She removed her panties and gently rubbed my swollen head against her opening. I groaned as I felt her wetness. I grabbed her hips, thrusting myself inside of her. I began breathing heavy after feeling her wetness envelope my warm, twitching cock.

"Harder, Terrell," she commanded as she moved her hips in circles. I thrust into her again and again. My hands gripped her waist as I raised my hips to meet hers, bouncing her while bouncing on the chair. I leaned over, kissing her chest as our bodies moved in sync. My lips captured her nipple between my teeth and the tip of my tongue. Sucking, licking, drawing her nipples and breasts into my mouth while moaning in pleasure as her fingers dug into my flesh. My moans make her bounce faster, pushing me deeper into her. Beads of sweat dropped as I felt my climax approach.

"I'm about to cum, Jen."

She whispered, "Cum for me." She let out a loud gasp as we both released together. My thick juices mixed with hers poured out of her warm puss.

Exhausted, we both reclined on the couch. I had missed her. I missed her touch. Maybe it's time to do the right thing. Maybe I should just let all the bullshit go. Dr. T was right. The anger, the rage, all of it was altering my personality. The guy I was wasn't the guy I used to be or wanted to be. Jen was a good woman. She was beautiful, smart and had a great career. I could see myself with her. I could see us together. It was time to make some changes.

Jen broke the silence asking,

"Do you want to go out tonight? We haven't really been on a date since that first night we met."

"Yeah, let's go out. I need to get out of the house. I have been stuck here for weeks angry."

"Angry about what?" she asked. "...and what's been going on with you? You still owe me an explanation."

She was right. I owed her an explanation. For the first time in a long time, I wanted to be completely honest. I began to tell her bits and pieces of sorted past. She listened intently as I told her how dark life got for me. She looked confused as I explained how the church can either build or destroy your faith. I talked about the turn my life took when love failed me. I thought I was going to run her away, but she stayed. I told her I wasn't a good person. I talked about my promiscuous ways with Yolanda and Ann Marie. I decided not to bring up the Kisi incident. Some things are just too disgusting to explain. Everything I said to her led back to my hatred of Bishop Prangles. I couldn't shake the thought that he was the root of it all. All the hurt, pain and bad decisions. All the confusion and lies. It was him. Prangles was a devil in the Pulpit. Before long, we were on our third bottle of wine.

"We better stop drinking if we are going out," she said.

"You're right."

"I'm going home to get dressed. Do you know where Posh Club is?"

"Yeah, I've heard of that spot," I said.

"Well that's where I want to go tonight."

"Okay, that's cool. What time do you want me to pick you up?" I asked.

"Let's just meet there around eight. I have to drop the kids off at a babysitter."

"Okay, that's cool." I walked her to the door. We kissed and embraced before she left. Holding her tight, I whispered in her ear, "I love you, Jen."

She pulled back from my embrace, smiled and said, "I know you do."

I watched her adjust her dress as she walked down the stairs. For the first time in a long time, I felt free. A weight had been lifted and I was ready to move on with life. It had been years since I experienced this feeling. I was happy.

I looked at my watch and it was 7:56. I was already in the parking lot waiting. I spent most of the afternoon fixing up some areas I had let go. I shaved my head and did some manscaping downstairs. Jen liked it smooth and I anticipated that she was going to get up close and personal. I got dressed and called Kareem to see if he wanted to be my wingman.

"What up, Kareem?"

"What's good, homie?"

"Chillin. Ain't shit happening. Bout to hit that Posh Club. You wanna ride?"

"POSH, man, I ain't going to that boujee club. You must be gonna be boo'd up?"

I laughed. I should have known he wasn't gonna come.

"Yeah, I'm meeting ol girl there." I didn't want to sound like I was whipped.

"Nah, bruh, imma hit Big Ratchet solo."

"Aight, Kareem, be easy. Hit me up if you need me."

"Cool."

We never went to Big City solo. There was always the chance that a fight would break out. That was the allure of Big City, it was ratchet. And every now and then you need a little ratchet in your life. I hung up with Kareem and finished getting dressed. I stepped out and caught a cab to Posh. I knew that Jen was driving so I planned on riding back with her. Plus, I wanted to drink. The cab driver dropped me off outside of Posh and I waited on the corner for Jen.

My mind was preoccupied with a car that resembled Kisi's and I didn't see Jen pull in. When I saw the lights from Jen black mustang, I figured my mind was playing tricks on me. I dismissed any thoughts of Kisi when I saw Jen. I watched her get out of the car. She wore fitted jeans, heels and a white Ralph Lauren shirt. I walked over to greet her in the parking lot. As I approached her, I leaned in for a kiss. She turned her head, suggesting I was gonna mess up her makeup. I loved her playfulness.

We walked in and sat down in a booth near the stage at Posh Club on the strip. It was Karaoke night and some chick was butchering Lauren Hill's *Nothing Even Matters. I* tried to contain my laughter. The club had a no heckling policy. It took all my strength not to be an asshole and boo her off the stage. Our waitress was prompt and took our drinks immediately. I had my regular Crown and Coke. Jen ordered Sex on the beach.

We listened and laughed at the parade of wanna be singers stumbling on stage. Jen convinced me to get up and by the time I was on my third Crown and Coke, I had no inhibitions. *Prince's Purple Rain* was my favorite song. I requested it and got up when the DJ motioned for me. As the music started, I noticed Jen leave the table. I sang my ass off. I knew every word and every run of the song. I had sung this song a million times. I knew every lick of the lips, every hip gyration and high note. I didn't get a standing ovation, but I didn't need one. I was the shit, and, in my mind, I killed the song.

"Fuck all them haters" is what I said to myself. "Them bitch asses don't know good singing when they hear it."

Just as I was walking off the stage, Jen made her way back to her seat. She was carrying her phone in her hand and I suspected she had to go out to use it. The club was loud, and I thought maybe she went outside to hear better. Probably it was her kids or the job, I thought. We were both in the army and are parents, so I knew that at any time she could get a call. I wasn't the jealous type so her leaving didn't really bother me.

As she sat down, I said,

"Hey, you missed my performance." I was used to her sarcasm but this time her response was cold.

"I heard you and it wasn't that good."

I said, "Well damn."

She seemed annoyed. "Terrell, we need to talk."

"Oh lord, any conversation between a man and a woman that starts with 'we need to talk' does not end well," I said.

She smiled. "You might be right because this one ain't gonna go good for you."

I had a puzzled look on my face. "What's going on Jen? Where is all this coming from?"

"Look, Terrell," she said bluntly. "I think I'm falling out of love with you."

"Wait a minute," I said. "Since this morning? We just had sex and I just bought dinner and drinks."

She said, "Yeah, I know and thanks."

My confusion grew greater.

"Jen, what's going on?"

"Terrell, separation could work out for the best. I didn't mean we wouldn't see each other. We can still fuck, I just don't want to be in a relationship. But we can still see each other every now and then."

My body went numb as a feeling of déjà vu fell over me. That's the same bullshit I said to Kisi. I stared at her, unsure if I should leave or see where this was going. This situation didn't feel right. Just as I was about to demand an explanation, Kisi walked over to the table.

"Oh shit!" My heart nearly stopped.

Jen laughed. "Why the 'Oh shit'? Do you know my girl Kisi?"

"Your girl?"

Kisi replied, "Yes, girls as in friends. Girls as in coworkers, you low down dirty dog. Did you know I had to move? I had five females come to my apartment looking for you. Two of them tried to push their way in, screaming your name. Security had to physically remove them, screaming out 'He cooked me spaghetti bitch' and laughing, talking about 'We fucked on the balcony.' My neighbors and coworkers live in that building. You are the lowest piece of shit. You took internet hoes to my house, you trifling ass nigga."

I wanted to apologize but I was speechless. How the hell had this happened? Why didn't I see this coming?

I looked in Jen's direction. "How long you been planning this?"

She said, "Not long. I didn't even know you two knew each other until you stopped taking my calls. I was talking to a friend of mine at work who happened to know Kisi. She recognized something similar in our misfortune. When I told her your name, she introduced me to Kisi. You are fucked up! Why would you do to someone what your ex-wife did to you? What kind of man brings other chicks to someone else's house?"

Before I could speak, Kisi interrupted.

"I had a feeling you were up to no good. Every time I came home, everything was perfect. Perfectly cleaned, perfectly washed, the house smelled fresh. Nothing was out of order. I should have killed you. I should have kept beating you in the heading with that pan until I fractured your skull."

The longer Kisi talked, the louder she became. Periodically, Jen grabbed her hand or pulled on her arm to let her know she was getting loud in this public place. I couldn't say anything, and they knew it. I had no more lies. I was caught, busted and exposed. So, I sat there and listened.

I looked at Jen,

"You are a good actress."

Sarcastically, she said, "Thank you."

Kisi chimed in, "She's a damn good actress. We fooled yo ass."

I looked at her and quickly looked away. I had already agreed to put my anger aside. And I was talking to Jen, not her.

"Jen, I tried to explain to you I was in a bad spot for a long time. I told you I wasn't a good person."

Kisi interrupted again. "Good person...nah nigga, you ain't shit. You talkin' bout you weren't a good person. What you need to be saying is 'I ain't shit...I wasn't shit...I still

ain't ahit. I ain't never gonna be shit. As a matter of fact, nigga, you less than shit."

I looked at her and quickly looked off again, reminding myself that I wasn't talking to her...I was talking to Jen.

"Jen, for the first time in a long time, I was straight up."

Kisi interrupted again. "It's too late, nigga. you over here beggin like Keith Sweat. You ain't shit, ain't shit."

Kisi was getting on my nerves. She was purposely trying to get under my skin. She was purposely trying to get a rise out of me. She was having her moment. Her moment of vindication. She was owed this moment. And as pissed off as I was at her disrupting my peace, I understood. I understood right up until she started singing her own personal version of an old Keith Sweat song:

And who loves you tonight? (Nobody)

Who are you sexting tonight? (Nobody)

Who can fuck up your night like me, me

baby? (Nobody)

Nobody, baby (Nobody)

And who can do it like me? (Nobody)

Who can give you what you need? (Nobody)

Who are you taking home tonight?

Nobody, baby!

I looked at Kisi, her smiling face filled with noticeable satisfaction. I couldn't be mad. I shouldn't be. I attempted to focus my attention back to Jen. She had a smirk on her face. A smirk that let me know this was over. I felt it. Nothing I said was gonna change this situation. Nothing I said was going to fix this. I thought to myself, I was in my apartment minding my own damn business and you pull me out of my house to embarrass me. Aww HELL NO! I stood to my feet.

"You know what, fuck this. And fuck you, Kisi. Yeah, I fucked bitches in your house and yeah, I cleaned everything... but guess what? I fabreezed them sheets. You slept in my cum and some other bitch's pussy juice."

Her voice quivered as she addressed Jen. "You see what kind of person he is? Let me introduce you to the real Terrell."

I continued. "Oh, so now you want to cry. You was Ms. Boss Bitch two seconds ago, rolling your damn neck, pointing your fucking finger and singing and shit. I got a song for yo

243

ass. *Who gives a fuck about you? NOBODY.* Fuck YOU! What are you gonna do? Unless you got a fucking frying pan in that purse, you need to get the fuck out my face."

My outburst was causing attention. The bouncer came over to deescalate the situation. Jen was silent. She stood up and grabbed Kisi by the arm and walked away. She had seen and heard enough. It really was over. I knew it and so did she. I watched them walk out of the club. I sat back down at my table. All eyes were on me and I could hear laughter as the next karaoke singer began her song. It was Gloria Gaynor. *At first I was afraid, I was petrified, kept thinking I could never live without you by my side, but then I spent so many nights thinking how you did me wrong, And I grew Strong and learned how to get along...*

I thought to myself, was this shit planned? Here is some random chick on stage singing with attitude. I guzzled my drink just as she went into the first stance of the hook, *Oh no not, I will survive Oh as long as I know love, I know that I am still alive. I got my life to live, and I've got all my love to give. And I...I will survive.*

I walked out to a chorus of every woman in the club singing along. It was the Woman's Anthem and I was that guy who made the song relevant. As I walked out, I turned and yelled, "FUCK ALL Y'ALL NO TALENT ASS HOES! Survive this BITCHES!" and stuck up my middle finger.

It wasn't my finest moment. I called a cab and waited on the corner. I saw Jen and Kisi still standing in the parking lot.

"Damn," I thought to myself, "that was her car." They looked as if they were consoling each other. I couldn't tell who was consoling who from their embrace. Jen glanced over and saw me watching and motioned Kisi to get in her car. They both pulled out of the parking lot, careful not to look in my direction.

My cab came about twenty minutes later. As I rode home, I began to reflect. I was hurt, alone and embarrassed. I was across the road. I could start fresh and move forward or I could be the same guy. Reasoning within myself wasn't easy. I knew who I used to be. I knew what type of man Momma raised me to be. Where did it all go wrong? When did I change? How did I change?

Prangles!

That's when it all started. That corrupt, no good, lying, fake ass preacher. I clenched my fist as a familiar feeling returned. I reached for my phone and called my oldest brother, Ron. I hadn't talked to him since that day I cussed him out. He picked up right away because he knew if I was calling, money was involved.

"Hey Ron, what's up?"

"What up, Boobie?"

I paused...I hated that fucking nickname. "I need a favor."

"What you need?"

"I need a gun, a clean gun, no bodies."

"Are you serious?" he asked.

"Yeah, I'm serious. I'm coming home, and I don't want

nobody to know. I need a gun. I will send you the money along with a...finder's fee. Do you still need that 150 dollars?" I knew he would try and screw me over.

"Nah, man, you know...um, that thing I had to do... because I was late, they charged me an extra hundred. So, I kinda need like 250 now. And you're gonna need to send about 100 for the gun," he said.

"WHAT? FUCK! You scheming ass, lowdown motherfucker." I thought to myself, this is the nigga I need to shoot.

"Alright, Ron, I will wire you the money. DO NOT TELL NOBODY I'M COMING HOME."

"Okay, Boobie, I got you. Give me about two weeks after you send the money. I know a guy, but he is doing ninety days on some bullshit simple possession charge. He's getting out the first of June."

I pulled the phone away from my ear and looked at it and said to myself, "This negro thinks I'm stupid." I wish he could see my face or feel my anger.

"Ron, it's April! The first of June is almost two months away, not two weeks. I swear dude, if you run off with my money, I will fuck you up so fucking bad, your kids won't know who you are."

He answered me quick. "I hear you, Boobie."

"You better hear me," I said. "I'll send the money next week and text you the information." I hung up.

Any other reputable brother would have tried to convince

me I was making an unwise decision. I didn't call my honest brothers. I didn't want to hear anything that sounded like common sense. I smiled as the driver pulled into my barracks complex. Walking up the stairs, a sense of calm swept over my body "I'm gonna kill Prangles, and I don't give a damn."

CHAPTER NINETEEN

The next morning, I got up early. It was Sunday. I looked at my phone expecting to see a missed call from Jen. She didn't call. My heart was hurting. I wanted to fix things so bad. I called her. My calls went straight to voicemail. I wasn't sure what to do. For the first time in a long time, my pride didn't matter. I wanted to talk to her. I didn't care what I had to do, I wanted to fix things.

Finally, I had found someone to make me smile again and this bullshit happens. I finally found someone that made me want to change. Jen was the type of woman I would do right for. She was the type of woman that only comes once in a lifetime. A part of me felt like this was karma. Maybe the universe had dealt me the hand that I had dealt so many. While sitting on my bed thinking, I uttered out loud, "Fucking Kisi, what the FUCK."

I dialed Jen's number again and again and again. Each time, it continued to go to voicemail. Maybe I need to give her some space, I thought. After-all, this crap did just happen last night. Maybe after processing everything for the next few days, she will at least allow me to talk and explain my side.

That thought was the only positive reflection I had. Every other thought was of me imagining Kisi reminding Jen of my bullshit daily. Or of her running to ask Jen if I had called or if she had talked to me.

"FUCKING KISI...what the FUCK!" I screamed.

I called a few more times then decided to occupy my mind with something. I volunteered to work extra shifts for anyone that needed time off. Jen wasn't going to talk to me, and the thought that maybe she never would bothered me. It consumed me. I decided to stop calling and texting and to write to her. I needed to make her understand that I wasn't the same guy. So, I began emailing her.

6 May 2005

Jen,

I laid down, and all I could think about was you rolling over and your body finding mine. I thought about you nestling yourself tenderly within the curve of my body in deep sleep. Your body always found my body. In my mind, I could feel your touch. The thought of you was so vivid I could smell the scent of your hair as you lay next to me. In my mind, I imagined looking at you while you rested. I like to watch you when you are asleep, not in some creepy-weirdo kind of way. I stare at the lines of your face, the hills and dips, your eyelashes, your breasts, your lips, the way your eyebrows get ruffled when your sleep is disturbed. You radiate innocence and seem at peace with the world, yourself, and perhaps, even me when you are asleep. It brings me comfort seeing you this way. It makes me smile when I remember you this way...at peace, without the stress of the world. I miss you. I miss you a lot. You were made perfect by God for me. You have a zest for life that is contagious, a smile that melts my heart, and a gentleness that warms my soul and a drive that inspires me. I love that about you and it makes me want to be with you forever. I'm sorry. I'm sorry that I hurt you. I'm sorry for the pain I caused you. I'm sorry that the tears I caused were not tears of joy. That guy that Kisi spoke to you about no longer exists. You made that happen. You made I want to be better. You made me want to turn my life around. I love you, can we please talk?

Always Terrell

10 May 2005

Jen,

Let me start by saying that I thank God every night since I found you. You came into my life when everything seemed so dark. You provided the light to help me find my way. I've never been so certain of anything in my life like I am of us. You have totally changed my outlook in life and I thank you for that. I never thought that someone could love me like you do, but guess what? I love you that much too. I feel as if I'm walking over clouds just thinking about you. You make my life complete. There is a saying that people do foolish things while in love, but you know what? With you, I wouldn't mind being a fool for the rest of my life. I love you so much and I know you love me too. Lately, I've been staring at your pictures, trying to figure out the right words to say to express these feelings I have inside. The words that will deeply but softly touch your heart and soul. The kind of words you've been wanting to hear for so long. Yet it seems useless when you don't respond or pick up the phone. That is why I decided to write you this letter. Silly of me to think it will change your mind, but it never hurts to try. Baby...I miss you. I miss you so much it's driving me insane hoping and praying you'll come back and give us another chance. I stayed up all night trying to figure out the right words. Then I began to think - What words would touch your ears like music, making you cry tears of happiness. Then it hit me. That I should just speak from my heart.

Ever since you walked into my life I have been smiling. There hasn't been a night when I have gone to sleep with a frown on my face, and it's all because of you, I am glad that you came into my life. I have always wanted the love of my life to be understanding, loving, caring, and faithful. I wanted someone who would accept me for who I am. I know that I've found that person in you. My heart told me that my princess was there when I first said hello to you. I didn't have to think twice when I asked you out. I knew that you were the perfect match for me. I don't think that there is, or that there ever could be, anyone better than you out there for me. I love you with my whole heart. I have never trusted anyone the way I trust you. Sometimes I even doubt myself, but I know I will never doubt you because you are my true love. I know deep down inside that you will never break my heart or let me down in any way...I'm sorry that I let you down. I can't change what I did in the past, I can only show you that I am a better man now. I can only show you this side of me. Jen I am ready for this, I am ready for love. Please allow me the chance to love you again. The stories you heard were stories! They were tales of a life that has passed away. I'm not proud of what I did to Kisi. Looking back on things I was stupid. Maybe I should apologize... although I know it won't make a difference. I know it will be looked at as if I had an ulterior motive. The only thing that matters to me is you. I love you Jenn.

Always Terrell

16 MAY 2005

Jen,

I know we haven't talked in weeks, but my feelings haven't changed. We both have gone through so much, and I feel like I relate to you on a much higher level than I have ever felt before. I think that if we take our time and do everything right, this love could blossom into a fairytale romance. All I ask, and I know I have said it before, is that you allow me to regain your trust. I have put all my trust in you, and I have opened every fiber of my being to you and only you. I want a future wife in my life, someone to hold, confide in, laugh with, and cry with; someone I can watch football with, walk along the beach at night with. I want it. I deserve it, as do you. I sincerely hope that you still feel the same as I do about us. You are beautiful, you leave me speechless, you turn tears into happy bliss, you make bad things seem not so bad. You brighten every aspect of my life. I have fallen in love with you. You are everything and more than what I have dreamed of my entire life. I know I am not perfect, but I do have goals in my life. I take good care of myself and my children. My love is honest, sincere, and true, and I have a lot of love to give if you are willing to be on the receiving end. I know that they say absence makes the heart grow fonder. I go to bed with tears every night waiting for the moment I can hear from you. I don't know this feeling. I have never experienced it. I want you by my side. I could never get tired of being near you whether on the phone, through emails or talking in person. I miss you more than words can say. I genuinely love you. I thought I would let you know that my love for you is burning very brightly this evening. My heart longs for you. My heart longs to leap at the sound of your voice. My heart longs to be filled with joy by your smile. My heart longs to be warmed when I hold you in my arms. My heart longs to feel the passion it feels as I caress your face, stare into your beautiful eyes and tenderly kiss you. My heart longs to see our love for one another grow as we sit on the couch and talk about having a life together. My heart longs for you Jen. All of me, Misses ALL of you. I love you.

Always Terrell

19 May 2005

Jen,

I am so completely in love with you. I wake to think of you and I sleep to see you in my dreams. Your love has made me love my life. Everyday seems like a blessing since I have met you. I feel so lucky and honored to be in love with you. Thank you for coming into my life and sharing your love with me. You are truly a wonderful gift. We both know what it's like to have a crush on another person and feel it slowly fade away as we get to know that person better. With you it's never even been in the realm of possibility for that to happen. My love for you has grown stronger and more real as time has passed. And I've felt my romantic heart grow in size and in strength too, so I know it's in there, and I know you feel it too. So, to say that I love you with all of my heart isn't just a clichéd romantic-sounding thing to say. To me, it means that my heart is full of love for you, and I promise to do everything in my power to maintain its commitment to you. I know we are facing a test right now. I call it a test because I know as time passes, we'll face other trials, but we'll also have beautiful, luminous times as well, and we will learn from everything that happens to us. This situation will not be the "Norm" of a life with me. I know you may fear that a life with me will be a continuous flow of disgruntled women emerging from my past. I promise you it won't be. As we love and learn, our hearts will grow better able to love each other and to give each other what we need to be happy. I can't live without you in my life. You are in my life, whether you know it or not. Images of you are always in mind. After you have left, your voice rings sweetly in my ears until I hear it again spoken from your own lips. Please Promise that I will not have to imagine you being near. Promise me that. Call it immature love; call it a crush; call it longing; call it infatuation; call it whatever you please. In my mind, I love you. When I love, I love forever. Please tell me that you love me, too. Please promise me forever. Please promise me that. Promise me you will always mine. There are a million things that come to my mind when I think of you and I know now that the reason why I'm so in love with you is because of how honest and true you are. You have never pretended to be anyone else and that's what made me trust you with all my heart and soul. You have made me feel secure again and that is the reason why I know that there could have never been another one for me. I hope you know just how much you mean to me my love, my heart beats only for you. I still remember vividly the moment that I first met you. I remember thinking to myself that I had definitely been hallucinating, for you seemed like a vision of perfection to me, so much so that I felt my heart frozen when you looked at me and smiled. I know it sounds like out of some cheesy romance novel but after all this while you still manage to take my breath away.

Always Terrell

22 May 2005

Jen,

I may not say I love you every day as some do. I may not have bought you beautiful gifts on occasions that matter. I may not have empathized when you were crying out for understanding. And I may not have done the right things to make you feel loved. If you are going to judge me on these things alone, I know I have failed miserably. But if only you could look through my heart to see who it is beating for, you would know the depth of my love for you. My emotions may not show but a love that is mostly hidden like mine is always deep and eternal. My heart can accommodate no other apart from you and I know this is how it is going to be for the rest of my life. True love resides in the heart just as how our love resides deep in mine. And no matter the seasons that will come and go, it will be there withstanding the test of time. As I write this today, the words are hard to flow. It is not my nature to be expressive. But no matter what, I want you to know that you are loved and cherished. And I want you to know that I do care. My words will never be able to describe exactly how I feel. When we first met, feelings that I didn't know existed stirred in my heart. An unexplained desire to know you better and a burning hope that I made a good impression. It is not often that we come across a person in our lives that we want him/her to take notice of us and ignite the spark that is embedded in our hearts. You are that person to me and my instinct has not been wrong. With each successive date, I come home with a stronger and stronger longing to make this last. A former belief that you are the one that I could share my life with. And a deepening love that reached a depth that I have never ever experienced. For some, love doesn't occur in an instant. I used to think that love takes some time to grow, especially the kind of deep love that envelops us now. But love can also be strange. If the person feels right in every way, love can take on a level of intensity that we never knew we are capable of feeling. Sometimes late at night, I lie in my bed and think about us. It has been such a miraculous ride, the kind that we never thought we'll be able to make through. I know that life is full of trials and that we cannot get what we want always, but I know that now that I have you, I can make it through any kind of situation that life might throw at us. Your love has filled me hope and has given me the strength to face my fears, which is something for which I shall be eternally grateful. Every night when we go to sleep, I listen to the beating of your heart. It is a sound that comforts me and makes me feel safe, at home again. Thank you love for being my strength, making me feel loved and ensuring that all my wishes do come true. The best thing about my life right now is you.

Always Terrell

Jen didn't respond to any of my emails. Deep down inside, I knew she wouldn't. She wasn't that type. She had seen bullshit before and understood that people show you who they are, and that initial first glimpse is what you should believe. What hurts is that I know that person Kisi told her about was not me. I showed Jen my vulnerable side. I showed her my heart and it wasn't good enough. It felt like I was destined to be in a bad situation. The thought of losing Jen hurt my heart. By the third week, I had plunged myself into a crazy work schedule. One day off, six days on. I worked my regular shift and filled in for anyone that wanted time off. I needed to stay busy. I needed to be occupied by something other than my thoughts. It was difficult sitting in my room. All I could think about was Jen. I didn't want to watch TV, but I didn't turn it off. I left it on all day because I didn't want to talk to anyone and I didn't want to sit in a quiet room. I just sat on the couch.

Blinking.

Staring.

Thinking.

The silence in my room was broken only by the hum of the Andy Griffith show theme song. Television was my comforter. I tried to stay busy as much as possible. When I wasn't busy, my mind wandered. Idleness of mind gives space for overanalyzing. And I scrutinized everything. I thought about where I went wrong. Maybe I should have told her everything. Maybe I shouldn't have left out the part about Kisi. Maybe I should have listened to Dr. T.

Was that exchange too much to come back from? Was she still upset? Maybe she was upset at me that day but remembers my good parts. Maybe because I didn't text her the last couple days, she misses me. Is she mad or afraid? Will she ever say anything to me again? I should call her and ask about it. But wait...no I shouldn't call. She needs space. Am I obsessing over nothing? Will she think I'm crazy if I call to talk about it?

I tried to think of what Dr. T would tell me. I could almost hear him saying, "*Well Mr. Terrell, most days the mind is ready and active to tackle the challenge of overanalyzing any situation, whether it be love, children, recent conversations or exchanges you have had with so-and-so, future plans, and more. There's never a lack of things to think about. But an idle, purposeless thought life creates a downward spiral of self-focused thoughts and fantasies about problems that aren't yet in existence or issues you can't control. An idle mind can very often be the devil's playground. You should find something to do.*"

I laughed at myself for trying to sound like Dr. T. Even in my imagination, Dr. T gave good advice.

CHAPTER TWENTY

The next day, I got up and went to work as usual. Sergeant First Class Meadows, my supervisor, noticed my crazy schedule. He called me in his office to see if I was okay. He knew that my step dad had passed and wanted to make sure that I wasn't overworking myself.

"Specialist Terrell, you love work so much you came in on your day off."

"It's not my day off. I'm filling in for another soldier."

He responded, "I know, that's why I called you in here. You are here around the clock. What's going on?"

Before I could speak, my phone vibrated. It was my brother telling me he had my package. I quickly changed the conversation. I needed to request time off. You have to put in leave ten days in advance. I would need special permission to take time off at short notice.

"Sarg, it ain't nothing going on. I'm glad you called me in the office," I said while slowly putting my phone away. Soldiers only talk to their NOC's when they need something or are in trouble. Neither of those made Sergeant First Class Meadows happy.

"You better not be in no shit!" he shouted.

"Nah, Sarg," I said. "I haven't been home in a while. My dad passed, and I didn't make the funeral. I just wanted to take some time to go check on family." He dropped his defenses.

"Family is important, and it might do you some good to get away. When do you want to g

o?" he asked.

"This week, Sarg."

"THIS WEEK! That's bullshit soldier," he yelled. "You know you need ten days advance to take fucking leave. What the hell kind of backyard horseshit you trying to pull? You are trying to leave this week. HELL NO!"

SFC Meadows was known for his rants. He could string together a barrage of profane words that would make the most experienced cusser take notes. I expected this response and made a counteroffer.

"Sarg, if I can find someone to work my schedule, then can I go? It won't be a hardship on the unit and I can get home to my family." He liked the idea of having someone to cover my shift. He knew that if we were short, it was his job to fill in and he hated working the ER floor.

"Okay, that will work, but I need it in writing," he said.

"Roger that, Sarg," I said with a smile.

"Don't fucking smile at me soldier. I ain't yo goddamn girlfriend. Now get your ass out of here on your day off before I put you to work. And quit working all them extra shifts, fuck you trying to do, make us look bad? Burnout is a real thing you know."

SFC Meadows had a way of showing he cared but maintained his asshole persona. Most of us knew it was an act. We knew he wasn't the hard ass he portrayed himself as. We went along with it. It's better to let him think we fear him then for him to know we don't.

So, I said,

"Roger that, Sarg, will do."

I left. I knew it would be easy to get people to work my shift. Money talked. I knew I would have to pay even though I had worked extra shifts for free. Niceness goes unpaid when it comes to labor. I spent the rest of the day calling fellow soldiers and making arraignments.

The next day on Monday morning, I went into work looking for Sergeant First Class Meadows. I handed him the written agreement between me and two other soldiers.

"How much did this set you back?" he asked.

It was illegal to pay soldiers to work for you. Sergeant First Class Meadows knew we did it all the time. Even though it was a common practice, no one ever acknowledged it, and I wasn't about to be the one who did.

"Sargent Meadows, that's an illegal practice. And I would never engage in something that unscrupulous."

He laughed. "Yo ass can't spell unscrupulous. When are you leaving?"

"I'm flying out Thursday morning. I want to be home before Friday night church service," I said.

My plan was to fly in, get my gun from Ron, get a hotel in Bamberg, then shoot Prangles during Friday night service in front of EVERYBODY. It was simple. No need for complications.

"Well, you got my number if you need me," SFC Meadows said.

"Roger that, Sarg."

I left and went back to my place to pack.

CHAPTER TWENTY-ONE

The week dragged along. My anxiety grew the closer it got to Thursday. I woke up filled with a calmness Thursday morning. It was an unexpected calmness. I grabbed my iPod and flipped to DMX. I didn't want to lose my heart or desire to do this deed. I wasn't sure what I should be listening to until DMX's *X-is coming* came on.

> 1, 2, X is comin' for you
>
> 3, 4, you better lock your door
>
> 5, 6, get your crucifix
>
> 7, 8, don't stay up late

I thought to myself, this is exactly what I needed to hear. This is the shit I needed to get me ready.

Who's afraid of the dark?
Responsible for the murders in the park
When I bark, they hear the boom, but you see
    the spark
And I see the part of your head which used to
    be your face
Leave you placed by nothin', for bluffin', what
    a waste
Niggas wanna see me taste my own medicine
Picture that, get on some old second grade
    shit, I'ma get you back
Retaliate, if it hates for you to think I took
    a loss
When all I did was shook it off
Yeah, you heard me, shook it off

I listened intently as I packed. I put my iPod on continuous play and allowed DMX to serenade me.

This is revenge, no time before you die
And despite how much I hate to see a grown
    man cry
I'ma make you suffer, see you in Hell,
    motherfucker

I thought to myself, "Yes I will I will see you in hell, Prangles."

I finally finished packing. I called a cab and got ready for my ride to the airport. I took a sleeping pill and ate a big meal before my eleven-hour flight. I wanted to sleep all the way. I boarded my plane and laid my head back, waiting for the pill to kick in. I was on a straight flight and I arrived at the airport in Columbia, South Carolina late. I didn't realize how much time had passed. I hadn't been home in almost three years. The divorce with Tanya was finalized and I had heard that she was already married again. I didn't care. Someone else could have that headache. My focus wasn't on her, it was on Prangles. My brother Ron was waiting for me at the airport. I greeted him with a partial hug. Ron pulled out a brown paper bag and handed it to me. I immediately became angry.

"Nigga, you gonna do this shit right here at the fucking airport. What the fuck? In front of the fucking police? Fucking TSA, TSO and the police out here and you gonna hand me a fucking gun in the parking lot. I swear, I think momma found yo ass."

Irritated at my comment he responded,

"Damn nigga." He angrily shouted back, "I was doing you a favor and yo loud ass is the one telling everybody you got a gun."

"How the fuck you doing me a favor? It's a fucking felony to have a gun at an airport.

Don't you watch the news? I swear you a dumbass," I responded.

We were brothers and we talked to each other anyway we

wanted to. Neither of us was thin skinned. Mamma didn't raise us that way. Someone listening would have thought we were about to fight but to us it was just a normal conversation. We got in his truck and I asked him to take me to Bamberg. I was already reaching in my pocket when he asked me to "help him with the gas." It was an hour drive to Bamberg. While en-route, I pulled the gun out and began to examine it.

"This shit is clean right?" I asked.

"Yup," he said.

"Ain't no bodies on it?" I asked.

"Nope," he said without looking at my facial expression.

I wanted to ask, "How come you aren't concerned?" I just flew eleven hours, asked him for a gun, and none of it fazed him. I knew that answer. That was Ron. He was who he was. We arrived in Bamberg at the only hotel in town. It was night and even though I slept all the way, I was still tired. I checked in and went back out to say goodbye. Ron was gone already. He knew I was up to no good and didn't want any part of it. I smiled. He is who he is.

I woke up at noon Friday morning. I was still jet lagged. I needed to get myself together. Church services started at eight pm and I wanted to be there. I went to the front desk and asked where the nearest car rental place was. He told me about a place called Zippy's about two miles away. I should have rented a car from the airport, but I didn't want to pay the fee. Somehow the cost of paying extra for car rental bothered me, but flying eleven hours to kill someone didn't. I walked down to Zippy's car rental. It wasn't a national car rental chain. This was a local guy who sold cars, fixed cars, rented cars and sold tires. It was also a gas station and a fried chicken restaurant.

I rented a 2005 Dodge Neon. I thought to myself, there was no way I was gonna outrun the police in this shit car. It didn't matter. I had no intention of running. I was ready to face whatever I had to face. I drove around Bamberg, trying to waste time before church. The local Bar B Que only opened on Thursday, Friday and Saturday. If I was going to jail, I was gonna do it with a belly full of chopped Barbecue pork. I pulled into Duke's BBQ and gorged myself on the buffet. Stuffed and satisfied, I made my way back to my hotel to sleep off the 'itis' that was coming down on me really fast. I made it to the room and laid down. As soon as my head hit the pillow, I was asleep again. The jetlag along with a belly full of pork had an effect on me.

I awoke to the sound of my phone ringing. The person hung up when I didn't answer. It was 7:30. I cursed myself for sleeping so long. The phone rang again. I answered. It was my brother Ron.

"What's up, Boobie?" he said.

I answered the phone angry. I thought he was about to ask for more money.

"What the fuck you want, Ron?" I scoffed.

"Man, Boo, I don't want nothing. I want you to hear me out though," he said.

"Okay, I'm listening," I said.

"Terrell, I have done a lot of things I ain't proud of. I have been to jail a few times, sold dope and been in some fucked up situations...but you ain't me. You don't do the shit that I do. You got a good head on your shoulders. Man, that army thing you are doing is the shit and I'm proud of you. I don't know what you're getting into or what you fixin to do...but man you ain't me. Don't be me man...keep being you. I wish I had made the moves you made. You are doing something, bruh. You are really doing it...you know what I'm saying? Be you man...don't be me. That's all I got to say." He hung up.

I knew what he was saying. I had never heard him talk like that before. Tears swelled in my eyes as I thought, "My big brother just did that."

All of these years of thinking he was a selfish asshole, and he was watching me the whole time. I sat on the side of the bed. My mind was racing. I came to the conclusion that he was still an asshole. I appreciated Ron, but I had a mission and I was going to complete it. No matter what.

I got up showered and put on some clothes. I grabbed my iPod and flipped to DMX. I was ready. I pushed out the thoughts of Ron's last message and any other positive thoughts. I took a deep breath, grabbed my gun and walked out to the car. It was 8:13. The church was only a few blocks away. I drove past the building, looking for Prangles truck. I knew where he parked and when I didn't see it, I knew he was running late.

"Probably out cheating on his wife again," I thought. Or maybe out spending someone else's money. I drove by a few more times, each time thinking about the long services. The embarrassment, being yelled at, misled, lied too, fooled and strong armed into doing shit I didn't want. At 8:41, I drove by again. He was there. My heart fluttered when I saw his truck. I looked in the mirror and screamed, "YESSS!" I turned around at the end of the road and drove back to the church. I pulled into the parking lot and pulled out the gun.

I sat in the church yard reflecting, thinking about all the pain. He was the cause of it all. If he would have told my Momma to leave that abusive relationship, she wouldn't be blind. If he wouldn't have manipulated the scriptures, I wouldn't have married that bitch of an ex-wife. I wouldn't be who I am. If he had just told the truth, things would be so much different. He ruined lives. He hurt people and he needed to die. He must die. I have to shoot this coward ass. I'm gonna blow his brains out right on the pulpit. Right in front of the church.

For years, I stopped going to church. I stopped listening to all the voices of people emanating from the church. I stopped listening to preachers, gospel radio and television, and I stopped reading material written by anyone in the religious system of the church. I loved church and he ruined it for me. I shared things with him that he said would "be between us and God." And not even a week later, half the congregation knew what I had told him. It was nine o'clock. I knew they were all inside. I knew that Prangles would be getting up soon to begin his long-winded sermon.

I blocked out any thoughts of mercy or compassion. I loaded my gun. It was time. It was time to end him. He was gonna feel pain. ALL OF MY PAIN! He was gonna know what hurt felt like. I was prepared for jail. I was prepared to smile everyday while locked up. I wanted him to die and nothing else mattered. I got out of my car and walked to the front of the church. My heart got heavy as I reached for the door. I could hear the choir singing.

I know somehow, I know some way we're going to make it. No matter what the test or whatever comes our way we're going to make it. With Jesus on our side things will work out fine, we're going to make it.

It was my mother's favorite song. Standing there at the church door with my 9mm Luger Semi auto-pistol, a flood of emotions ran through me. A moment of clarity. "I can't do this." My Momma, Dr. T, they all had been trying to tell me the same thing. Let it go. I sat down on the steps, listening to the choir.

Some way somehow, we're gonna make it.

I thought about how my Momma forgave the man that took her vision. She even forgave Prangles. She let it all go. As I sat there thinking about the past an enormous amount of clarity washed over me.

I said out loud, *"God I need help."* I stood up, shaking my head and began to walk back to my car. Walking away, I heard a voice say, "If you need help, you've come to the right place." I felt nauseous. I knew that voice. My rage was renewed. I knew that voice. I didn't immediately turn around. Something within me said, "Just walk away." But I couldn't. I didn't. I turned to see Pastor Prangles standing there in his pinstripe navy blue suit.

"Deacon Terrell?" he said. I fumed inside. I hated that name.

"That's not my name." The words rolled off my lips with venom. I wanted him to feel my rage. I wanted him to feel my anger. But he didn't...he couldn't. His ego and narcissism wouldn't allow him to think that anyone hated him as much as I did. I clenched the gun handle tight. I asked God for help and here I was, standing here staring at the source of my rage.

"I'm sorry, son, but you will always be Deacon Terrell to me."

His voice provoked me. It vexed my soul.

"TO YOU?" I said, seething with a frenzy of rage. I continued, "I am nothing to you...none of us are. We are not people, we are objects. Objects for you to toy with...objects for you to control. Well, you don't control me, not anymore."

"Deacon Terrell," he interrupted.

"That's not my FUCKING NAME!" I screamed.

"Now, wait a minute son. I'm still a man of God, show some respect for the house of the lord."

"House of the LORD?" I laughed sarcastically. "Old man, this is your house. God ain't nowhere in it."

"Son, you are still disrespectful, and I will not tolerate that from you or anyone else. If you want forgiveness, you need to come inside. The altar is still where it was when you ran away from God."

As he turned to leave, I thought to myself, "He hasn't changed. He's still the same egotistical, self-centered bastard." And I as watched him turn to walk away, the only thing I could muster was a loud,

"NO." I raised the gun and pointed it at him.

"You brought a gun to God's house?"

"No," I said. "I brought a gun to your house."

"Dea—" I interrupted him before he finished.

"If you call me Deacon Terrell, I swear I will blow your fucking brains out on those church steps," I seethed.

"Okay, okay, just calm down son," he said.

"Son!" I screamed. "ARE YOU TRYING TO DIE?"

"No, no, no," he said, putting his hands up. "Just calm down, Terrell. Why all this anger? What did I do to you?" he asked.

I couldn't believe he asked that. I hated him for years and he asked, "What did I do?"

"What the fuck do you mean, what did you do? You lying, no good, manipulating piece of—" I stopped. I needed to calm down. I needed to have this conversation in clarity. I was committed to pulling the trigger. I needed him to know why. I needed to make him see what he had done. So, I paused and gathered myself. Then I spoke:

275

"I despise every single thing about who you are—the person. You are evil, and you don't even know it. You are a curse. Your very existence on this earth is a burden. People walk in fear of you. I saw it in everyone. They were nervous. We all were nervous. We all walked on eggshells hoping we didn't piss you off. Hoping that we wouldn't experience a long service that singled us out. You saw that fear. You fed off that fear. And you bashed us mercilessly. We all felt like we deserved to be treated badly. Like this is what God wants. I know I did. I thought that God wanted me to be under your foot. I thought God wanted me beatdown by you."

"Wait a minute, Terrell," he interrupted. "I encouraged you. All I wanted to do was bring you closer to God."

"HOW!" I yelled. "Does it look like I'm closer to God? Does it look like any of us are closer to GOD? My Momma was beat blind, and you told her God wanted her to stay. My step dad beat us all and you told us to honor him. All it took was one word from you and we would have left. Momma would have walked away. She didn't have faith in Harry she had faith in you. I BELIEVED IN YOU! People right here in this church are living in poverty, paycheck to paycheck, cars breaking down in the church yard and you just drive off in your new Suburban or Tahoe or Hummer. You're a coward who hides behind the pulpit. You deserve to die." Tears flowed from my eyes like raindrops. My soul emptied as the words fell from my lips.

"You want to kill me?" he asked.

"No," I interrupted. "I'm going to kill you." I walked closer to him, pushing the gun to his chest. Everything within me said, "Do it!" Everything within me screamed, "Pull the trigger!"

"Terrell," he panicked. "Hear me out first." I paused. I wanted him dead, but I also wanted to know why. Why did he treat us so badly? Why did he dog us out so bad? Why? So, I took a step back and lowered the gun.

"Okay, I'm listening," I said in a huff.

"Terrell, I'm not perfect. I never claimed to be perfect. When I met you, I was young in the ministry. When you came here, you were young too. I was trying to teach you all the best way I could. I was trying to tell you about God the way I was taught. I made mistakes, but we all have. Church is a place to change and to grow. I have grown. I had no idea you felt this way. If I would have known you had these feelings towards me, I would have reached out."

I couldn't believe what I was hearing. How the hell did he not know? How could he be so fucking clueless? He destroyed my morale. He destroyed my faith and now he sits here saying he didn't know. He didn't know he broke me. He didn't know that I married that sorry ass woman. All these years I hated him, and he didn't know. How is that possible? How could he not know?

I spent years imagining him laughing at the pain he caused me and my family. I never once even considered he was young or didn't know. Nah, he was in charge, he was the

Preacher, he was in charge and HE'S responsible. I looked down at the ground trying to make sense of this. My hatred for this man shaped everything in my life. I lived in hate. I was stuck, and I never moved forward. I couldn't. I wanted revenge. I wanted him to hurt. More than anything, I wanted him dead.

And then I looked back at him.

"You are a liar! You know what you did!" I yelled.

"Terrell," he pleaded. "I didn't know."

Listening to him plead made me hesitate. I thought about what he was saying. This moment was the first time I had a thought about Prangles that wasn't pure hate. I held the gun tighter and tighter. My heart was saying no but my head was saying shoot his ass. He sensed my hesitation. He sensed my reluctance. I looked into his eyes. Looking at him I could see his sincerity. I could feel his honesty. What was this feeling? I didn't want to pity him. I didn't want to have empathy. No, no, no, no...He deserves to die for what he's done. He deserves to suffer. His family deserves to suffer. I struggled within. All of my anger and all of my rage had accumulated to this one moment.

I closed my eyes and said,

"You know what, I don't fucking care if you knew."

I pulled the trigger, expecting to hear the boom of my weapon discharging. *Click.*

Nothing happened. I looked down at the gun and pulled the trigger again. *Click.* I feverishly pulled the trigger. *Click,*

click, click. As I looked down at the gun, my eye caught the sudden lung of Prangles. Our eyes met as he rushed towards me with fists clenched. Stepping back, I swung both fists connecting with Prangles face. It stunned him, causing him to hesitate. He wasn't expecting that.

"You hit me!" he yelled. "The Bible says, 'Touch not my anointed and do my prophet no harm.'"

I laughed. "You are not anointed, and I think God is on my side in this one." At that moment, I felt an awakening. I wasn't going to kill him. He wasn't worth it. Nah...killing him was easy. I didn't want to kill him. I wanted to whip his ass. I ran towards Prangles with rage in my eyes. I couldn't shoot him, but I could pistol whip his ass.

Grasping my gun in the palm of my hand, I swung, striking Prangles again in the face. He fell back, grabbing my shirt, pulling me toward the ground. I fell on top of him. Sitting up, I straddled him and proceed to reign down the blows to his face. I could feel the blood soak my fist as I pummeled him repeatedly. For a brief moment, I considered his age. Here I am, a 30 something year old man beating the crap out of a 50-year-old preacher. Fuck it. He earned this ass kicking.

I grabbed him around the throat, pressing my hands firm against his carotid artery. I watched his eyelids get smaller and smaller. I was choking the life out of him and it felt good. My hands were locked in. Unbeknownst to me, some members of the congregation heard the commotion. The doors of the church opened. Three of the church brothers ran towards me as I was sprawled over Prangles with my hands around his neck. Grabbing me, they pulled me off Prangles. Before I could stand to my feet two of the brothers began kicking and stomping while the other brother tended to Prangles. I stood, trying to get my balance and mount a defense against two stooges who were beating the shit out of me.

I didn't know these guys. They were new. They came after I had left. They knew of me. They had heard my name several times. Mark and Lionel took up the task of restraining me. Mark was a correctional officer. He had some police training in restraint. He knew a few pressure points that he attempted to utilize on me. Mark wasn't a big guy. He was average size with eyes that looked like he was constantly surprised. I had never seen eyes protruding from someone's face like he did. Lionel was slim. Nothing about him was intimidating. Lionel was ugly. Not unattractive...UGLY.

I was embarrassed. I was getting my ass kicked by a pop eyed freak and a dude whose face resembled a Baboon's ass. Mark grabbed my arm flipping me to the ground. I rolled over landing on the gun that was dropped. I picked it up as Prangles tried to walk up the church stairs. The remaining church members began to file outside. I picked up the gun and stood to my feet. Prangles saw me standing, holding the gun.

He yelled to Mark and Lionel,

"That gun don't work."

Backing up, I dropped the magazine from my gun. I looked at it and quickly re-inserted it. I cocked it and pulled the trigger. BOOM. The loud blast shocked everyone. It stunned me. There was a strange silence. Everyone froze. I turned the gun towards Prangles.

"It's working now," I said.

He stood there, silent as the rest of the congregation pleaded for me to leave. They loved him as much as I hated him. They adored him as much as I despised him. One of the church mothers stepped out from behind the crowd. It was Mother Dukes. She walked over to me, leaned over and said, "That's enough."

She put her hand on my hand and repeated, "Terrell, that's enough." My heart felt heavy. Her motherly presence caused tears to flow. I lowered my weapon. Mother Dukes was taller than me. She extended her arms and hugged me tight. My body went weak. I cried in her arms. Mother Dukes hugged my pain away. She held me there. I didn't notice the other members leaving. I didn't see Bishop Prangles leave. Mother Dukes stepped back and looked me in my eyes.

She said, "Terrell, it's over now. Let it go."

I had heard that several times from my own mother. Dr. T told me to let it go several times. This was the first time I listened.

"Terrell, you have to forgive and let it go. You have to try. You're better than this. Be better."

"Yes, ma'am," was all I could say. I knew she was right. My body felt lighter. A weight was gone. And I needed to leave it alone.

"Thank you," I said.

She smiled and asked, "Are you coming to church?"

I laughed and said, "That might not be a good idea."

She smiled and said, "You're probably right."

I hugged Mother Dukes again and walked off to my car. Before I got in, I paused, took a deep breath and took one last look at the old church. As I sat in the car, I pulled out my phone. Driving out the parking lot, I dialed Dr. T. I forgot that there was a six-hour time difference between South Carolina and Hawaii. Dr. T. answered immediately.

"Hello?"

"Hey, Dr. T. Its Terrell."

"Good evening, Terrell. Is everything okay?"

"Yes, sir, everything is fine. I wanted to make an appointment to continue our sessions next week."

"Terrell, I think that is an awesome idea. I will make a note and have Nancy call you with the schedule."

"Thanks, Dr. T. You have a good evening."

"You too, sir."

ABOUT THE AUTHOR
RYAN T. MOORER

I fell in love with writing in the 7th grade. Mrs. Collier, my 7th grade English teacher, was instrumental in helping me develop my passion for this art. As a writer I have worn many hats, Father, Husband, Son, Brother, Soldier and Cancer Survivor. I began this book when I was diagnosed with Stage VI Colon Cancer in 2018. I began to write everyday while receiving Chemotherapy, radiation and other immunotherapy.

Emily Dickinson wrote, *"To be alive is POWER"*! I believe you can't let life happen to you, you have to make life happen. Doors close and opportunities pass, but life goes on. **Writing gave me power. Writing gave me life.**

Made in United States
North Haven, CT
17 June 2022

20320744R00163